INSIGHT ⊙ GUIDES

EXPLORE

PARIS

PLAN & BOOK
YOUR TAILOR-MADE TRIP

BRAZIL

CHILE

ECUADOR

TAILOR-MADE TRIPS & UNIQUE EXPERIENCES CREATED BY
LOCAL EXPERTS /HOLIDAYS

Insi... ...uality travel
...lebooks,
w... ...ate trips
...sts.

By c... ...ctly benefit
...u create

ORKS

STEP 1

Pick your dream destination and submit an enquiry, or modify an existing itinerary if you prefer.

STEP 2

Fill in a short form, sharing details of your travel plans and preferences with a local expert.

STEP 3

Your local expert will create your personalised itinerary, which you can amend until you are completely satisfied.

STEP 4

Book securely online. Pack your bags and enjoy your holiday! Your local expert will be available to answer questions during your trip.

BENEFITS OF PLANNING & BOOKING AT INSIGHTGUIDES.COM/HOLIDAYS

PLANNED BY LOCAL EXPERTS
The Insight Guides local experts are hand-picked, based on their experience in the travel industry and their impeccable standards of customer service.

SAVE TIME & MONEY
When a local expert plans your trip, you save time and money when you book, even during high season. You won't be charged for using a credit card either.

TAILOR-MADE TRIPS
Book with Insight Guides, and you will be in complete control of the planning process, from the initial selections to amending your final itinerary.

BOOK & TRAVEL STRESS-FREE
Enjoy stress-free travel when you use the Insight Guides secure online booking platform. All bookings come with a money-back guarantee.

WHAT OTHER TRAVELLERS THINK ABOUT TRIPS BOOKED AT INSIGHTGUIDES.COM/HOLIDAYS

Trip to Portugal

Every step of the planning process and the trip itself was effortless and exceptional. Our special interests, preferences and requests were accommodated resulting in a trip that exceeded our expectations.

Corinne, USA

Trip to Vietnam

The organization was superb, the drivers professional, and accommodation quite comfortable. I was well taken care of! My thanks to your colleagues who helped make my trip to Vietnam such a great experience.

Heather

DON'T MISS OUT BOOK NOW AT INSIGHTGUIDES.COM/HOLIDAYS

CONTENTS

ART ENTHUSIASTS

From the big three – the Louvre (route 2), Musée d'Orsay (route 3) and Centre Pompidou (route 5) – to the more intimate Musée Rodin (route 3), Musée Jacquemart-André (route 4) or Monet's house in Giverny (route 19).

RECOMMENDED ROUTES FOR...

CHILDREN

Try boating in the Tuileries or Jardin du Luxembourg (routes 2 and 8), combine the zoo and the dinosaurs at the Jardin des Plantes (route 7) or head out of the capital to Disneyland (route 20).

CLASSIC CAFÉS

Take it easy with the bohemian crowd in the Marais (route 6) or sip coffee like the existentialists at Les Deux Magots and Café de Flore in bourgeois St-Germain (route 8).

ESCAPING THE CROWDS

Find a quiet corner at Père Lachaise cemetery (route 11) or head off the beaten tourist track to the up-and-coming northeast (route 12) or the smart 16th *arrondissement* (route 14).

FOOD AND WINE

The 7th (route 3), home to some of the city's best restaurants, the Champs-Élysées (route 4) for Ladurée macaroons, rue Mouffetard (route 7), with its vibrant food market, or Bercy's former wine warehouses (route 13).

LITERARY TYPES

Pay homage to Victor Hugo in the Marais (route 6), rifle through racks of antiquarian books in the Latin Quarter (route 7) or visit Balzac's house in Passy (route 14).

PARKS AND GARDENS

Take a break in main parks such as the Tuileries and the Luxembourg (routes 2 and 8), or sample less well-known green spaces including the impressively planned Parc des Buttes-Chaumont (route 12).

SHOPPERS

The department stores on the Grands Boulevards (route 4), the boutiques of the Marais and Bastille (route 6) and the bookshops of the Latin Quarter (route 7).

INTRODUCTION

An introduction to Paris's geography, customs and culture, plus illuminating background information on cuisine, history and what to do when you're there.

Young doodlers at the Berges sur Seine

EXPLORE PARIS

With two World Heritage sites, over 200 museums, more than 420 parks and gardens, and nearly 200 churches and temples, it's not surprising that Paris's population of 2.2 million have to share their good fortune with around 16 million visitors a year.

Paris is a comparatively compact city and more suited to walking than many, particularly for a capital. The city runs for 13km (8 miles) east and west, around 9km (6 miles) north and south, and is contained by the Périphérique, a ring road that is famous for its traffic, which runs 35km (22 miles) around it. The suburbs *(la banlieue)* form two concentric rings around Paris, and are split into *départements* or counties.

RIVER SEINE

The city is cut through the middle by the River Seine, which is spanned by 37 bridges. The river is the city's calmest – and widest – artery, barely ruffled by the daily flow of tourist and commercial boat traffic. It enters Paris close to the Bois de Vincennes in the southeast and meanders gently north and south past three small islands: Île St-Louis, Île de la Cité and, on its way out, Île des Cygnes.

Chains of hillocks rise up to the north of the river, including Montmartre (the highest point of the city), Ménilmontant, Belleville and Buttes-Chaumont (*butte* means 'hill'); and, to the south, Mont-souris, the Mont Sainte-Geneviève, Buttes aux Cailles and Maison Blanche.

CITY LAYOUT

One of the most persistent images of Paris is of elegant long avenues lined with huge chestnut and plane trees. Chains of broad boulevards encircle the centre of the city, marking where the boundary was in medieval times. Many of the capital's streets contain the word *faubourg*, indicating that they were once part of the suburb outside the city wall.

Arrondissements

In fact, the capital is organised into *arrondissements* (districts), which spiral outwards in a neat snail-shell pattern from the Île-de-France (the 1st *arrondissement*) to the northeast (the 20th). All of these are contained within the Périphérique ring road. When Parisians explain where they live, they typically begin with the number of their *arrondissement*. Within these areas are recognised *quartiers*, or neighbourhoods, each of which has a distinctive character.

Time out in the Jardin du Luxembourg

TRADITIONAL DIVIDES

According to an old saying, the Left Bank (south of the river) was where you did your thinking – the Sorbonne university has been located there since the Middle Ages – and the Right Bank (north of the river) was the place to spend money. Yet, in addition to this historic divide, there is a marked unofficial division between the traditionally working-class eastern end of the city and the mostly bourgeois west. In general, the further east you go, the further left you will also find yourself on the political spectrum. City planners have been struggling for decades to redress the social imbalance, culminating in urban-renewal projects around the Bastille (see page 52) and in Bercy (see page 82).

POPULATION

Central Paris is more densely populated than London or New York, with its residents squeezed into tiny apartments in the city's 87 sq km (33.5 sq miles). A house and garden is an almost unheard-of luxury, and there is intense competition for desirable living space, with an average of 150,000 people looking for a home at any one time. High rents, especially in the western *arrondissements*, add to the fact that many Parisians have neither the time nor the money to appreciate the city they live in, being locked in a routine that they describe as *métro-boulot-dodo* (commuting, working, sleeping).

Nonetheless, for anyone who is fortunate enough to live in the city centre, the rewards far outweigh the demands. Human in scale, clean, cosmopolitan and lively, Paris lives up to its reputation as one of the best cities for living the good life. Sadly the French capital hasn't been immune to terrorist attacks, and the whole country is on high security alert ('plan Vigipirate'). Always remain alert in major tourist centres.

CULTURAL SCENE

Paris dominates the country's art, literature, music, fashion, education, scientific research, commerce and politics, despite concerted attempts in recent years at decentralisation in France. It may not be good for the country as a

Family values

As part of the government's policy to encourage population growth in France, each *famille nombreuse* (i.e. with three children or more) is rewarded with benefits including nursery provision, subsidised public transport, sports equipment, car tax and school meals, and free admission to museums. The birth rate, which had been declining for years, is now on the rise. The National Institute for Statistics now measures the rate at more than two births per woman; this increase has been boosted by France's large Muslim community.

whole, or for the provincial cities, but it adds to the cultural richness of life in the capital. Little wonder that the writer Jean Giraudoux (1882–1944) once claimed that the Parisian was more than a little proud to be part of a city where 'the most thinking, talking and writing in the world have been accomplished'.

ARCHITECTURAL DEVELOPMENT

Largely undamaged by two world wars, Paris is the result of centuries of grandiose urban planning. It escaped only by a whisker during World War II, when General Dietrich von Choltitz, the occupying governor of Paris, defied Hitler's orders to destroy every single historical edifice in the city as the Allied troops approached.

Gothic and Renaissance styles
However, little remains of the city's architecture prior to the Gothic period. The 12th-century west front of Notre-Dame (see page 28) is a fine example of early Gothic, while the transept with its intricate tracery and the interior of Sainte-Chapelle (see page 27) are excellent examples of mid-13th-century High Gothic.

In the mid-16th century, following campaigns in Italy, François I introduced grand Renaissance forms to the French capital. The best example of the French interpretation of the Renaissance style – known as Mannerism – is the palace at Fontainebleau (see page 96).

Baroque and Neoclassicism
In the first half of the 17th century 60 new monasteries and 20 churches were built in the capital, with the aim of turning it into a second Rome. Churches such as Val-de-Grâce, in the 5th, were modelled on the Roman Baroque template with a two-storey pillared facade, a broad, barrel-vaulted nave flanked by chapels, and a high cupola above the crossing.

French art entered its classical phase in the reign of Louis XIV (1643–1715), notably with the palace of Versailles (see page 92). Louis Le Vau, Jules Hardouin-Mansart and Charles Lebrun designed the exterior and interior, while landscape architect André Le Nôtre laid out the formal gardens.

The same team was appointed to oversee changes to the city, removing the city walls, replacing the old gates with triumphal arches, and redesigning place des Victoires and place Vendôme as royal squares with statues as centrepieces. The Louvre was extended, and the addition of the Tuileries and the Champs-Élysées created a 'Royal Axis' (see page 32).

The 19th century
The storming of the Bastille in 1789 heralded the start of the destruction of many churches during the years of revolution. However, Napoleon brought reconstruction and extended the Royal Axis by adding the Arc de Triomphe.

By the 1860s, though, neglect and rapid urban growth had made Paris ripe for redevelopment. Under town plan-

The Louvre and its glass pyramid

ner Baron Haussmann, the residential quarter of the centre was pulled down, the street system transformed, and parks laid out on the outskirts. The bourgeois pomp of the period reached its apogee in architect Charles Garnier's opera house (see page 46), while mercantile success found expression in international exhibitions, notably that of 1889 which brought with it the Eiffel Tower (see page 38).

Early 20th century

The Modern Movement of the 1920s and 1930s and Art Deco, characterised by clean lines and stylised forms, were born in Paris, with architects Robert Mallet-Stevens and Le Corbusier their

---

DON'T LEAVE PARIS WITHOUT...

Finding a good boulangerie to sample its freshly baked delights. Buy some still-warm croissants or pains au chocolat and find a leafy square nearby to eat them in. Alternatively, head to macaroon-specialist Ladurée to sample one of its mouthwatering creations. See page 47.

Having a coffee in a typical Parisian café. There are many to choose from: take your pick from the historic, and touristy, Café de Flore; Chez Prune, in the trendy Canal St-Martin area; or Le Procope, the oldest café in Paris (1686). See pages 65, 81 and 62.

Seeing the city from the river. Begin at the city's origin, the River Seine. Make your way to the western tip of the Île de la Cité, via the steps down from the Pont-Neuf. From here, take one of the Vedettes du Pont-Neuf boat tours and glide along one of the most enchanting river journeys in the world. See page 129.

Strolling in the Jardin du Luxembourg, the most elegant of Paris parks. You'll be in good company alongside joggers, boules players, statues, and smooching couples. See page 65.

Getting a towering view over Paris. Climb up the Eiffel Tower for the quintessential viewing experience. If you want to capture the Eiffel Tower in your shot, then head to the top of the Arc de Triomphe. If it's atmosphere you're after, make your way to Montmartre in time for sunrise – or sunset – and savour the panoramic view over the city from the Sacré-Cœur's front steps. See pages 38, 32 and 67.

Getting a culture fix. There is of course the unmissable Louvre, but also try and take in one of the smaller, more intimate showcases such as the refined Musée Rodin, the exquisite Musée Jacquemart-André or the cutting-edge Palais de Tokyo. See pages 30, 40, 43 and 72.

Shopping till you drop. Paris is the fashion capital of the world and there is something for everyone here, from the elegant Belle Époque *grands magasins* of Printemps and Galeries Lafayette to the cutting-edge fashion and design boutiques of the Marais and the genteel galleries and passages near the Palais-Royal. See page 20.

Jardin du Luxembourg sculpture

chief exponents. At the same time, a more grandiose, neoclassical form of Modernism emerged, epitomised by the Palais de Chaillot (see page 73).

Later 20th century

From the 1960s, Paris underwent a transformation. Facades were cleaned, the metro network modernised, and old parts of the city, such as the market at Les Halles (see page 50), demolished. Technical advances enabled architects to build upwards (La Défense, see page 88), expand indoor space (Centre Pompidou, La Villette, Bercy, see pages 48, 78 and 82) and experiment with materials that reflect and admit light.

In the 1980s François Mitterrand left his mark with a number of *grands projets* (see page 31). These include I.M. Pei's pyramidal entrance to the Louvre (see page 32), Jean Nouvel's Institut du Monde Arabe (see page 61), the Opéra Bastille (see page 57), Grande Arche at La Défense (see page 89) and the Bibliothèque Nationale de France (see page 83).

The 21st century

Recent years have brought Jacques Chirac's Musée du Quai Branly (see page 39), while Nicolas Sarkozy also intended to assure his legacy through architecture as well as infrastructure. His 'Grand Paris' (Greater Paris) scheme kicked off with a pledge of €35 billion for a swish new suburban transport system and he invited 10 world-class architects, including Jean Nouvel and Richard Rogers, to draw up their visions of a more cohesive Greater Paris. New skyscrapers (long banned in central Paris) are under construction – work on Sir Norman Foster's Hermitage Plaza in La Défense began in 2019; at 323m (1,059ft), it will be the European Union's tallest building upon completion in 2024. Another high-rise, the Triangle Tower, is scheduled for 2020.

New museums and extensions of existing museums have also opened in recent years: the new Department of Islamic Art wing of the Musée du Louvre, designed by Rudy Ricciotti and Mario Bellini, in 2012; the Frank Gehry-designed Fondation Louis Vuitton 'landed' in the Bois de Boulogne in 2014 and in 2015 the new Philharmonie de Paris welcomed its first music lovers. In 2019 the old Bourse de Commerce in the newly revamped Les Halles district will reopen as the Collection Pinault – Paris.

As Paris prepares to host the 2024 Olympic Games, it has to deal with the ongoing, and now country-wide, "gilets jaunes" anti-austerity movement. And in April 2019, Paris was dealt a severe blow when the much-loved Notre-Dame Cathedral dramatically caught fire. The structure was saved but the roof and spire were completely destroyed. President Macron has vowed to rebuild it in record time "more beautiful than ever", thanks, in part, to an outpour of donations – so watch this space.

Inside the Musée de l'Orangerie

TOP TIPS FOR EXPLORING PARIS

Nuit Blanche. 'White Night', or cultural all-nighter, is held on the first weekend in October. Paris stays alive until the wee hours of the morning, with museums, art galleries and other cultural institutions opening their doors for free all night long. Special events are also organised across the city. Some metro lines run all night long on a Nuit Blanche to help sleepy punters get home.

La politesse. The widespread Parisian reputation for rudeness is largely undeserved; in fact, many locals follow strict rules of etiquette, and visitors are advised to follow the standard. Whether you are buying a baguette or shopping at Chanel, starting any transaction with a '*Bonjour Madame/ Monsieur*' and finishing with '*Merci, au revoir*', for example, should make the world of difference to the service you receive.

Museum pass. If you plan to visit several museums during your stay, buying a Paris Museum Pass enables you to avoid the queues and save money on entrance prices at over 50 museums and monuments in Paris and the Île-de-France region; you can also make unlimited visits within the time allowed. Cards are available for two, four or six days and can be purchased from tourist offices, museums and galleries, at the airports and online (www. parismuseumpass.com).

Jazz in Paris. On rue des Lombards (2nd) are three of Paris's most famous jazz clubs: Le Baiser Salé, Le Duc des Lombards and the Sunset/Sunside. The Parc Floral inside the Bois de Vincennes has free jazz and classical concerts on summer weekends.

À vélo. One of the best ways to explore Paris is by bicycle. Borrow one for free through the Velib' scheme (see page 124).

Avoid the queues at Versailles. Book tickets for the palace in advance via www. chateauversailles.fr. One of the simplest tickets is the Passport, which gives admission to the main sites. EU residents under 26 years old (non-EU under 18 years) are admitted for free.

Taking the train to Fontainebleau. The SNCF sells an all-in-one train-bus-château ticket. Check train times before travelling (www.sncf.fr), as services are infrequent.

Vaux-le-Vicomte. You could combine route 18 with a visit to the palace at Vaux-le-Vicomte (Maincy; www.vaux-le-vicomte.com; Mar–Nov 10am–7pm, for more information visit the website), as the two are within 16km (10 miles) of each other and on the same train line. Vaux is the former home of Louis XIV's one-time Finance Minister, Nicolas Fouquet, and generally considered to be the forerunner to Versailles.

Beat the crowds at Giverny. Monet's house and garden can be extremely crowded with coach parties and school visits so aim for an early morning or late afternoon visit. You can also buy your ticket online to save queuing time (www. fondation-monet.com).

Rustic cuisine with an elegant twist

FOOD AND DRINK

French food is, of course, not all snails and frogs' legs. Its attractions include oysters, foie gras, bœuf bourguignon, steak tartare, coq-au-vin, and sole meunière. And then comes dessert: tarte tatin, mousse au chocolat, îles flottantes, and so much more.

Paris has the reputation of being one of the best cities in the world for food, with an illustrious gastronomic history. You may not find the most experimental dishes here, and the approach to food is admittedly far more conservative than, for example, in London or New York, but this is not without its benefits, especially for those visitors in search of classic French cuisine.

CONTEMPORARY AND INTERNATIONAL

This is not to say that contemporary and international cuisines cannot be found. In recent years, young chefs have been opening more fashion-conscious restaurants – impervious to Michelin ratings – serving French food, yet integrating (cautiously) more exotic flavours, such as ginger, peanut, curry and lime.

The international scene, although not as widespread as elsewhere, is also an integral part of the city's food culture. The greatest concentrations of Chinese and Vietnamese restaurants are in the 5th and 13th *arrondissements* (the Latin Quarter and southeast to the new Left Bank), while Japanese eateries are concentrated in the 1st (Louvre, Palais-Royal and Châtelet).

The best Moroccan restaurants are peppered across Paris, but around the Bastille is a good place to start. There is excellent Lebanese food in the 8th and 16th (Madeleine, Grands Boulevards, Champs-Élysées and West), while good African food can be found around Pigalle and the East.

PLACES TO EAT

Brasseries
Brasseries (breweries) were introduced to Paris in the 19th century, at about the time when modern methods of brewing were being perfected. They're a jolly experience: spacious, clamorous and convivial, usually exuberantly decorated in Belle Époque style. Many serve Alsatian specialities, such as *choucroute* and steins of beer; others specialise in seafood. Outside, you can usually see heaps of shellfish on beds of ice, and men in overalls shucking oysters from dawn till dusk. Usefully, unlike most other restaurants in Paris, brasseries generally remain open on Sundays.

Traditional brasserie   *Many brasseries specialise in shellfish*

Bistros

On the whole, bistros are smaller-scale establishments and mostly offer variations on a traditional repertoire of dishes including *hareng pommes à l'huile* (smoked herring marinated in oil with warm potatoes), *blanquette de veau* (veal in a white sauce), *mousse au chocolat* and *tarte tatin* (caramelised apple upside-down tart). A number of bistros have a regional bent, and offer provincial specialities such as *foie gras* and duck (southwestern), hot pepper, salt cod and ham (Basque), and *bouillabaisse* (Provençale).

In the past few years, a new breed of restaurant has been springing up in Paris: the 'néo-bistrot'. A response to the economic crisis, néo-bistrots are usually run by young chefs, cost significantly less than one might expect, the cuisine is innovative and cosmopolitan, and the atmosphere relaxed. In 2015, Le Chateaubriand (129 avenue Parmentier, 11th; tel: 01 43 57 45 95; Tue–Sat dinner only), which has a daily changing menu with international influences, was voted the 21st best restaurant in the world and earned itself a Michelin star even though many critics once claimed this would never happen.

Cafés

These, in the traditional sense of the term, usually serve sandwiches, notably the ubiquitous *croque-monsieur* (grilled ham and cheese), as well as a variety of giant salads, quiches and omelettes. Some establishments offer fuller menus with a Mediterranean slant and more elaborate, modern dishes.

High-end restaurants

Whether Michelin-starred or not, this category ranges from the gloriously old-fashioned, with truffle-studded *foie-gras* terrines and venison in grand sauces, to the self-consciously cutting-edge, with hot pepper sorbets to cleanse the palate between veal slow-cooked in orange juice and desserts that show off fruit or chocolate in five different ways. Such restaurants often have tasting menus *(dégustation)*.

Michelin stars are taken very seriously in France. At the time of print-

Vegetarians and vegans in Paris

Vegetarian and vegan dishes of French cuisine are more prevalent than before and more and more places are springing up in Paris which cater for non-meat eaters, mostly in the form of hip eateries. If you find yourself in a traditional restaurant though, order two meat-free starters instead of a main course, or stick to simple egg and potato dishes. In an upmarket restaurant, you can telephone ahead and request a vegetarian meal; this gives the cook time to concoct something just for you. Another option is to explore the city's ethnic restaurants, which serve meat-free snacks as well as elaborate three-course meals.

Néo-bistrots have spruced up the cooking scene

ing, Paris had 9 restaurants with three stars, whereas London, for example, had only three, and New York had five. Losing a star can mean a sharp decline in the number of a restaurant's customers as well as a dent in the chef's pride.

Markets

In general, visiting Parisian food markets is a morning activity, with stalls opening at 9am and packing up at 2pm. Of the daily street markets, the Marché d'Aligre (place d'Aligre, 12th *arrondissement*; Tue–Sun) has an indoor part (the 'Marché Beauvau') with produce of the highest quality (and price), as well as a noisier, cheaper outside section. At the market on rue Mouffetard in the Latin Quarter, look out for the Italian delicatessen, Facchetti, and their famous baker. Among the roving markets are Saxe–Breteuil (starting from place de Breteuil, 7th; Thur and Sat), with specialists in snails, wild strawberries and foie gras; Bastille (flowing from place de la Bastille, 11th, up boulevard Richard-Lenoir; Thur and Sun), with stands devoted solely to onions, mushrooms, honey or eggs; and Belleville-Ménilmontant (boulevard de Belleville to boulevard de Ménilmontant; 11th and 20th; Tue and Fri), with exotic varieties of peppers, giant watermelons, Chinese cabbages and flatbreads made from rye or barley.

CHEESE

Between the main course and dessert comes the cheese trolley or platter, laden with a delectably smelly array. There are two rules which may be helpful: 1) In a cheese tasting, always start with the mildest cheese and work your way around to the strongest; and 2) Never steal 'the nose' off a piece of cheese if you're serving yourself; always slice cheese in such a way as to preserve its natural shape. This is considered proper behaviour, since it means that the last person served will not be left with just the rind.

The French are the world's fourth biggest consumers of cheese after Denmark, Iceland and Finland: approximately 27.2kg (59lb) per person per year. Many cheeses taste a lot better than they look; some goats' cheeses, for example, are coated in charcoal ash, as this absorbs surface moisture and helps preserve them.

Varieties

The number of varieties means that it can take years to become familiar with French cheeses. President Charles de Gaulle once said, 'how can you govern a country that has 246 different kinds of cheese?' In fact, cheese in France is as regulated a produce as wine, with a similar Appellation d'Origine Contrôlée (AOC) classification system, as well as a protected 'Designation of Origin'. There are currently over 40 cheeses with AOC status (Roquefort was the first, in 1925), and in total

Plenty of cheese   *At the Marché d'Aligre*

somewhere from 350 to 400 varieties of French cheese.

DRINKS

Alcoholic beverages

It is common to be offered an *apéritif*, such as a glass of Champagne, white wine, a kir (white wine with the blackcurrant liqueur, cassis) or sometimes white port, before a meal in France.

Wine is the ever-present accompaniment to eating, though, whether by the bottle, by the glass or, cheaply, by the jug. In bistros, brasseries and cafés, though often not in formal restaurants, house wine can be ordered in *carafes* or *pichets* (earthenware jugs). Quantities are normally 25cl (*un quart*), 50cl (*un demi*), or sometimes 46cl (*un pot lyonnais*).

The current trend in France is to drink less wine, but of better quality. The interest in organic wine has also mushroomed – Cyril Bordarier's Le Verre Volé (see page 120), by the Canal St-Martin, is a *cave à manger* (a fashionable cross between a wine cellar and restaurant), specialising in organic wines. Recent years have seen a growth in Parisian restaurants focusing on wine, including quite a few of the Michelin star recipients. France constantly vies with Italy for the title of world's largest wine producer, and two-thirds of the annual production of 600 million cases is consumed in France; expect, therefore, to find relatively few bottles from overseas on restaurant wine lists.

Beer is usually only ordered with sandwiches, Alsatian meals or Asian food; artisanal beers by the city's first microbrewery, Brasserie de la Goutte d'Or, are sold at numerous bars and restaurants including Le Verre Volé. Cider accompanies Breton and Norman specialities such as *crêpes* or mussels, and is often served in earthenware beakers.

After dinner comes the *digestif*, which may be a glass of Cognac, Armagnac, Calvados, or distilled fruit liqueur.

Soft drinks and coffee

Numerous mineral waters will be on offer in most restaurants. Request *pétillante* for sparkling; *plate* for still; or *en carafe*, if you are happy with a jug of tap water.

Coffee in France is usually served after, rather than with, dessert. *Café* means espresso, strong and black. If you like milk, request a *café noisette*. *Café crème* (coffee with milk) is considered a breakfast drink; ordering it after dinner may raise eyebrows. Finally, if caffeine is likely to keep you up all night, ask for a *café décaféiné* (*déca* for short), or for *une tisane* (herbal tea).

> ## Food and drink prices
>
> Throughout this book, the price guide is for dinner for one person with half a bottle of house wine:
>
> €€€€ = over 60 euros
> €€€ = 40–60 euros
> €€ = 25–40 euros
> € = under 25 euros

Galerie Vivienne

SHOPPING

While Napoleon once branded Britain 'a nation of shopkeepers', nowadays the phrase is more aptly applied to France, and viewed not as an insult but as a compliment for the wonderful array of one–off specialist boutiques and stores.

In an age when shopping seems to be an increasingly uniform experience wherever you are, with the same international groups and luxury labels in every major city around the world, Paris still retains its tradition of family-owned specialist shops, and chain stores and *centres commerciaux* (shopping malls) are far less prevalent here than in most other European capitals.

Most shops open from 9 or 10am until around 7pm. Few stores open on Sunday, except in the Marais and a few on the Champs-Élysées. Some smaller shops close on Monday all day or in the morning until about 2pm. Many close throughout August for the traditional French summer holiday. The main sales *(soldes)* periods in France are January and July.

THE SHOPPING MAP

The city's different *quartiers* each have their own mood and atmosphere, and their shops often reflect the history and type of people who live there. Expect to find shops selling classic and expensive items (antiques and upmarket interior design as well as fashion labels, for example) in the wealthy, fairly conservative 7th

and 16th *arrondissements*, and bohemian designers and independent gift shops and boutiques on the hilly streets of Montmartre (rue des Abbesses, for example), in the fashionable Bastille and Marais, along rue Étienne Marcel and dotted along the banks of the Canal St-Martin.

Couture and chains

The city's big couture houses are clustered mostly in the avenue Montaigne area (off the Champs-Élysées), the Faubourg St-Honoré and St-Germain. When the world's first ever concept store, the much-loved Colette, closed in 2017, ex-staffers opened its successor Nous in rue Cambon, a street eponymous with Chanel. Even the exclusive avenue Montaigne has tempered its bourgeois image with the arrival of hip young labels Shiatzy Chen and Zadig & Voltaire; all of which has had the knock-on effect of attracting other cool boutiques and gift shops to the area.

Tradition and change

Emblematic of glamour in the early part of the 20th century, the Champs-Élysées nose-dived to tourist dross in the 1980s. Its return to favour at the end of the 1990s was confirmed by the arrival here

The Faubourg St–Honoré is seriously chic

of *pâtissier extraordinaire*, Ladurée (see page 47), and in the last few years the avenue has been boosted by a swathe of swish concept stores.

In the past decade, designer stores have migrated to St-Germain, much to the chagrin of those who bemoan the loss of the district's distinguished book-sellers and literary cachet.

The once widely disliked Forum des Halles shopping centre reopened in 2016 after an extensive five-year rede-velopment. A curved canopy now hov-ers majestically over 120 shops, 22 restaurants, 34 cinema screens, an Olympic swimming pool, a media cen-tre and, outside, landscaped gardens.

Not that every area is in the throes of regeneration. The aristocratic past of boulevards Bonne Nouvelle and Mont-martre is a dim memory blurred by the ranks of discount stores and high-street chains that now dominate the area.

That said, the department stores, or *grands magasins*, built in the 19th century, still hold their own and look as impressive as ever. Indeed, the Galeries Lafayette, Printemps and Le Bon Marché – home to trendy, emerg-ing labels – are worth a peep for their architecture alone.

GALLERIES AND PASSAGES

In the 1840s Paris had over 100 pas-sages, or covered arcades, built with shops below and living quarters above. They were places for Parisians to dis-cover novelties and the latest fashions, while protected from the elements. Nowadays there are only around 20 left, mostly near the Palais Royal. The pas-sages usually open from around 7am to 9 or 10pm, and are locked at night and on Sunday.

Highlights

The best-preserved gallery, **Galerie Vivienne** (5 rue de la Banque, 2nd), has a beautiful mosaic floor and gorgeous iron-and-glass roof. This fashionable spot is home to the ateliers-boutiques of Jean-Paul Gaultier and Nathalie Garçon, art galleries and the genteel A Priori tearoom.

Galerie Véro-Dodat (19 rue Jean-Jacques Rousseau–2 rue du Bouloi, 1st) dates from 1826 and is perhaps the finest of the passages, with wood-and-brass shop fronts and carved Corinthian capitals. Highlights include leather goods at Il Bisonte and bespoke make-up at By Terry.

Passage du Grand Cerf (10 rue Dussoubs or 145 rue St-Denis, 2nd) is probably the coolest of the arcades – something of a creative headquar-ters. Come here to admire work by cut-ting-edge graphic designers, milliners and jewellers.

Passage des Panoramas (10 rue St-Marc or 11 boulevard Montmar-tre, 2nd) is one of the earliest of the arcades, opened in 1800, and above all a focus for philatelists, with half a dozen specialist stamp dealers.

The storming of the Bastille, 1789

HISTORY: KEY DATES

The Parisii tribe discovered it, the Romans conquered it, the Franks invaded it, and Napoleon ruled it. The city's refined culture and revolutionary politics changed the world. The list below covers major, mostly political, events.

EARLY HISTORY

c. 300 BC   Celtic Parisii tribe settle on the Île de la Cité and found Lutétia.

58–52 BC   Paris conquered by the Romans; building on the Left Bank.

451   St-Geneviève saves Paris from Attila the Hun.

508   Clovis, King of Franks, makes Paris his capital.

THE MIDDLE AGES

987   Hugues Capet is elected king; start of Capetian rule.

1253   Founding of the Sorbonne.

1340   Hundred Years' War begins.

1420   Paris surrendered to the English, who rule until 1436.

RENAISSANCE AND ENLIGHTENMENT

1515–47   Reign of François I, during which he starts to rebuild the Louvre.

1594   Henri IV converts to Catholicism, ending the Wars of Religion.

1682   Louis XIV moves his court to Versailles.

REVOLUTION, EMPIRE AND REPUBLIC

1789   French Revolution ends centuries of monarchy, which is replaced by the First Republic. Louis XVI and Marie-Antoinette are executed in 1793.

1794   The ensuing Terror claims more than 60,000 lives.

1799   Napoleon Bonaparte seizes power and is crowned emperor (1804).

1814–15   Fall of Napoleon heralds the restoration of the Bourbon monarchy.

1830   Bourgeois revolution; Louis-Philippe of Orléans becomes king.

1852   Louis-Napoleon crowns himself Napoleon III: the Second Empire. Baron Georges Haussmann begins an 18-year redesign of the city. The

Boulevard Haussmann in the early 1900s

city's first department store, Le Bon Marché, opens.

1870–1 Franco-Prussian War. Paris surrenders. Napoleon III abdicates. End of the Second Empire.

1871 Uprising by the Paris Commune, with 25,000 people killed.

1889 Eiffel Tower built for the World Fair. Pigalle's Moulin Rouge opens.

20TH CENTURY

1900 First Paris metro line opens.

1914–18 World War I.

1939–45 World War II. France falls to the Nazis in June 1940. Paris is liberated in August 1944.

1946 Charles de Gaulle founds the Fourth Republic.

1958 Algerian crisis topples the Fourth Republic. De Gaulle founds the Fifth Republic. Women are finally given the vote.

1968 Student riots and workers' general strikes rock Paris and force de Gaulle to call an election. He wins but resigns a year later.

1969–74 Georges Pompidou's presidency.

1981–95 Mitterrand's presidency is notable for his *grands projets*.

21ST CENTURY

2002 The euro replaces the franc as the French unit of currency.

2010 President Sarkozy unveils his plans to create a 'Greater Paris'.

2012 Socialist François Hollande elected president.

2014 Paris elects its first female mayor, Socialist Anne Hidalgo.

2015 7–9 January: terrorist attacks on the Paris headquarters of *Charlie Hebdo* satirical magazine and a kosher supermarket by Muslim extremists kill 17 people and injure dozens. 13 November: another series of attacks by Muslim extremists on Parisian cafés, the Bataclan concert hall and the Stade de France kills 130 people and injures 368.

2017 Emanuel Macron is elected French president.

2018 France win the FIFA World Cup for a second time, beating Croatia 4–2 in the final. Later that year, the anti-austerity "gilets jaunes" movement begins its Paris protests.

2019 On 15th April a major fire ravages through Notre-Dame Cathedral, resulting in the roof and main spire collapsing. Paris is the main host city of the FIFA Women's World Cup held in France.

2024 The 2024 Summer Olympics are scheduled to take place in Paris from 26 July to 11 August 2024.

BEST ROUTES

The Conciergerie

THE ISLANDS

The two largest islands in the Seine – the Île de la Cité and the Île St-Louis – offer up the full span of the history of Paris, via some of its greatest sights: the Pont Neuf, Notre-Dame, the Conciergerie and Sainte-Chapelle.

> **DISTANCE:** 2km (1.25 miles)
> **TIME:** Two or three hours
> **START:** Pont Neuf
> **END:** Île St-Louis
> **POINTS TO NOTE:** Notre-Dame is closed until further notice following the 2019 fire.

It was on the Île de la Cité, the largest island in the Seine, that the city of Paris was founded by the Celtic Parisii tribe in the 3rd century BC. The island remains the geographical centre of the capital, though the focus nowadays is tourism, which is mainly to view Notre-Dame (currently closed for extensive renovations but the structure is still visible).

PONT NEUF

This route starts on the **Pont Neuf ❶**, which, despite its name (New Bridge), is actually the city's oldest. Henri III laid the first stone in 1578; Henri IV inaugurated the completed bridge in 1607.

Lunch 'en terrasse'

Statue of Henri IV

As you walk south across the bridge, note the equestrian statue of Henri IV. Originally produced in 1614 under the orders of Marie de Médicis, Henri's widow, it was destroyed in 1792 during the Revolution, then rebuilt in 1818 on the monarchy's restoration.

Behind the statue are stairs leading to **square du Vert-Galant**, a tiny patch with views across to the Louvre and a good place for a picnic. Across the road is the **Taverne Henri IV**, see .

PLACE DAUPHINE

Adjacent to the Taverne Henri IV is an opening on to **place Dauphine ❷**. This square was commissioned by Henri IV in 1607 in honour of his son, the dauphin Louis (later Louis XIII), and intended as a market for traders. It is now lined by 32 elegant white-stone townhouses around a triangular courtyard.

Cross the square and turn left on to the quai de l'Horloge, named after the city's first public clock, which is on a tower of the Conciergerie.

THE CONCIERGERIE

The **Conciergerie ❸** (2 boulevard du Palais; www.paris-conciergerie.fr; daily 9.30am–6pm) was originally part of the palace of King Philippe the Fair (1268–1314), but quickly became the residence of the keeper of the royal palaces or *comte des cierges* (keeper of the seals), from which the word *concierge* is derived.

The building was later transformed into a prison, and it was here in 1793, during the Reign of Terror, that around 2,600 of the condemned spent their last night before facing the guillotine. Now a museum, the Conciergerie has a guillotine blade on display, as well as the crucifix Marie-Antoinette used at prayer while in captivity here, and the lock from Robespierre's cell.

SAINTE-CHAPELLE

Concealed in the courtyard between the Conciergerie and Palais de Justice (the French supreme court) is the Gothic **Sainte-Chapelle ❹** (4 boulevard du Palais; www.sainte-chapelle. fr; daily Apr–Sept 9am–7pm, Oct–Dec 9am–5pm, Jan–Mar 9am–5pm). The chapel was built in the 13th century to house holy relics, including Christ's Crown of Thorns.

Colourful blooms at the Marché aux Fleurs

Enter via the lower chapel, which was used by palace servants. Note the star-patterned ceiling. Stairs lead to the upper chapel, where light blazes through 15m (49ft) -high stained-glass windows separated by the slimmest of buttresses. Those interested in chamber music should check the bulletin boards for concert schedules.

THE MARCHÉ AUX FLEURS

Cross the road to place Louis-Lépine. Here, at the **Marché aux Fleurs Reine Elizabeth II** ❺, flower-sellers ply their trade from Monday to Saturday, while on Sundays caged-bird sellers take their place. Continuing east across rue de la Cité is the **Hôtel Dieu**, the oldest hospital in Paris. Founded in the 7th century, it was rebuilt by Baron Haussmann in the 1860s. Adjacent is place du Parvis Notre-Dame, in front of the cathedral.

NOTRE-DAME

The building of **Notre-Dame** ❻ (place du Parvis Notre-Dame, 4th; www.notreda medeparis.fr; currently closed following a fire; reconstruction is expected to take until 2024, at the earliest) was initiated by Bishop Sully in 1163, and took almost 200 years to complete.

In the centuries since, it witnessed medieval executions, a conversion to a food warehouse during the Revolution, the coronation of Emperor Napoleon in 1804, and the service marking the Liberation of Paris in 1944 (interrupted by sniping and wounding of several of the congregation), and most recently the devastating 15 April 2019 fire.

Although the roof and spire were completely destroyed and the upper walls damaged, the bulk of the cathedral was spared. The famous 13th-century stained-glass rose windows, iconic bell towers and 18th-century Great Organ (the largest pipe organ in France), as well as much of the cathedral's priceless artworks and religious artefacts were saved, due to both the building's stone-vaulted ceiling, which protected the interior, and the bravery of Paris's firefighters, 500 of whom fought the blaze for over five hours, pumping water directly from the Seine river.

At the time of publication, no direct cause has been attributed to the fire, however there has been speculation that it stemmed from the renovation work that was on-going at the time.

Less than 48 hours after the fire, over one billion US dollars was pledged from around the world to rebuild Notre-Dame, which President Macron vowed to complete in time for the 2024 Paris Olympics (though experts estimate the reconstruction could take more than 20 years). In the weeks following, the French prime minister launched an international design competition for a new spire. A May 2019 poll showed that nearly 60 percent of people wanted any rebuilt spire to be identical to the original.

Berthillon, worth queuing for

East of the cathedral is the **Mémorial des Martyrs de la Déportation** ❼ (Apr–Sept Tue–Sun 10am–7pm, Oct–Mar until 5pm; free), a monument to those deported to German concentration camps in World War II.

ÎLE ST-LOUIS

From the memorial, take the pedestrian bridge to the **Île St-Louis**. Follow rue St-Louis-en-l'Île along the spine of the island past a succession of grand mansions interspersed with boutiques and restaurants. The Hôtel du Jeu de Paume at no. 54 was once a real tennis court. Hôtel Chenizot at no. 51 has a splendid rocaille doorway with bearded fauns, and a balcony supported by dragons.

When you reach rue des Deux-Ponts, turn right for a moment to see the **Pont de la Tournelle** with Landowski's 1928 Art Nouveau statue of the patron saint of Paris, St Geneviève.

Back on rue St-Louis-en-l'Île, you soon come to the Baroque church of **St-Louis-en-l'Île** ❽. Designed by Louis Le Vau in the 1660s, it is notable for its open-work spire, iron clock and 16th- and 17th-century artworks.

Island of Cows
Perpendicular to rue St-Louis-en-l'Île is rue Poulletier (formerly Poultier), once a fortified canal, with the area beyond having been a boggy pasture known as the 'Island of Cows'. In 1614, it was filled in and transformed into an elegant residential quarter. At the end of rue St-Louis-en-l'Île, at no. 2, is the Hôtel Lambert, built by Le Vau in 1641 for Louis XIII's secretary.

Quai d'Anjou
Now turn left and double back on yourself to find the **Hôtel Lauzun** ❾, at 17 quai d'Anjou. Built in 1640 by Le Vau, the mansion was home in 1845 to the poets Théophile Gautier and Charles Baudelaire, who wrote his collection *Les Fleurs du Mal* here.

Finishing the route here, turn right and cross Pont Marie to the metro. Alternatively, pop into **Berthillon**, see ❷, for their much-fêted ice cream.

Food and drink

❶ TAVERNE HENRI IV
13 place du Pont-Neuf, 1st; tel: 01 43 54 27 90; daily 8.30am–11pm; €€
Diminutive spot offering straightforward French cuisine and excellent wines. Try the eggs baked with blue cheese and ham, washed down with a white Beaujolais. Excellent value given the high-profile location.

❷ GLACIER BERTHILLON
29–31 rue St-Louis-en-l'Île, 4th; tel: 01 43 54 31 61; Wed-Sun 10am-8pm; €
Parisian ice-cream institution (est. 1954) with an attractive tearoom next door.

The Louvre old and new

LOUVRE AND TUILERIES

The Louvre is arguably the most famous museum in the world, with claims to also being the largest. There are 35,000 pieces of art on display (from a collection of 460,000) in 6ha (15 acres) of exhibition space, so after your visit you may need to rest on a deckchair in the pretty Tuileries gardens.

DISTANCE: 1.5km (1 mile), not incl. distance covered in museum
TIME: A full day
START: Louvre
END: Jeu de Paume
POINTS TO NOTE: If the pyramid entrance to the museum is congested, enter instead at 99 rue de Rivoli, via the Carrousel du Louvre shopping centre, or directly from the metro. With a Paris Museum Pass (see page 15), you can go in via the Porte des Lions entrance. Tickets are valid all day, which allows re-entry into the museum after a rest in a café or restaurant (or even the Tuileries) outside the complex. Note that the museum is closed on Tuesdays and that entry is free on the first Saturday of each month from 6–9.45pm.

This tour incorporates a morning in the **Musée du Louvre ❶** (rue du Louvre; www.louvre.fr; Thur and Sat–Mon 9am–6pm, Wed and Fri 9am–9.45pm), followed by an afternoon in the adjacent Tuileries gardens. If you need somewhere to have breakfast, try the **Café Marly**, see ❶, or, if you're visiting later in the day, **Le Fumoir** or **Le Garde-Robe**, see ❷ and ❸.

LOUVRE BACKGROUND

Originally built as a fortress in 1190 by King Philippe-Auguste to protect a weak link in the city wall, the Louvre was transformed into a royal château in the 1360s by Charles V, who established his extensive library in one of the towers.

Sections of the palace were demolished, rebuilt or extended by successive monarchs, including François I, who in 1516 invited Leonardo da Vinci to be his court painter; the Italian brought with him his masterpieces the *Mona Lisa* and *The Virgin of the Rocks*, now highlights of the museum's collection. In 1682, however, the Louvre's period as a royal palace came to an end, as Louis XIV decamped entirely to Versailles.

Artists move in

Following the court's departure, a colony of painters and sculptors moved into the Louvre's empty halls and corridors; among them was Guillaume Coustou, sculptor of the *Marly Horses*, now one of the Louvre's most prized exhibits.

During the 18th century, the fine arts academy, which had joined the Académie Française and other academic bodies in the royal apartments, organised exhibitions in the Salon Carré for artists to exhibit their work. This became the tradition known as the 'Salon' and lasted for over 120 years.

Public museum

During the 18th-century Revolution, in a moment of artistic enthusiasm, the Assemblée Nationale decided to inaugurate the palace as a museum, ironically fulfilling the plans of Louis XVI, the king they had just beheaded. Opened in August 1793, the museum exhibited the collections of the royal family and of aristocrats who had fled abroad.

These were augmented by Napoleon's efforts to relocate much of Europe's artistic wealth here following his victorious military campaigns in Italy, Austria and Germany. After Napoleon was defeated at the Battle of Waterloo in 1815, many of the stolen masterpieces were reclaimed by their rightful owners, but many more remained.

The rest of the 19th century and the first half of the 20th century brought with them periodic upheavals, notably the 1830 and 1848 revolutions, the Franco-Prussian War, the Paris Commune and two world wars, yet the Louvre continued to expand its collections and gradually came to occupy the whole of the vast complex of buildings.

Grand projects

The culmination of this process came in 1981, when President François Mitterrand commissioned a massive renovation of the Louvre, as one of his '*grands*

The Louvre's Egyptian Antiquities collection is the largest of its kind

projets'. When it was finished, the so-called 'Grand Louvre' had doubled in size, giving it claim to being the world's biggest museum, with 6ha (15 acres) of exhibition space. It also became the world's most visited museum, with more than 8 million visitors per year.

The pyramid

The controversial Louvre pyramid, designed by Sino-American architect I.M. Pei, opened in 1989. For some, it reflects and complements the ancient curves of the surrounding buildings. However, to traditionalists such modernism amid heritage is heresy.

The pyramid forms part of the Royal Axis, or Triumphal Way, an alignment of monuments, regal and triumphal, leading from the Louvre's Cour Carrée via the Arc de Triomphe du Carrousel and Arc de Triomphe to the Grande Arche in La Défense. Contrary to popular myth, its steel structure does not contain the satanic number of 666 panes of glass, but 673 segments.

But the pyramid was not just designed to dazzle. It also allows light to flood into the new sunken court housing the main ticket desks and, along with three smaller pyramids, illuminates the area where shops, restaurants, cafés and an exhibition area are situated.

Latest developments

In September 2012, the Louvre opened a new section to house the Department of Islamic Art. Designed by Rudy Ric-ciotti and Mario Bellini, an iridescent, undulating roof covers 2,800 sq metres (30,000 sq ft) of exhibition space set over two floors underneath the Cour Visconti. The main patron was Saudi Arabian businessman Prince Al-Waleed bin Talal who donated $23 million (£15 million) towards the project.

TOUR OF THE MUSEUM

The museum itself is divided into three wings: **Richelieu** in the north, **Sully** in the east and **Denon** in the south. The collections are displayed in colour-coded sections, to help with orientation, and floor plans are also available at the ticket desks. The following is a brief tour, showing what is displayed where, including information on the highlights from the different sections.

The Medieval Louvre

You start at the lower ground floor of the Sully Wing, where the remains of Philippe-Auguste's fort and keep built in 1190 are on show, as well as some of the artefacts discovered in excavations in the 1980s. Drawings and scale models show the Louvre at different stages of its evolution, and reveal how many transformations it has undergone.

Walk around the medieval walls and fortress, past towers that were once the gates to the city then head to the Department of Islamic Art in the Denon Wing.

Under the glass pyramid   *Veronese's massive 'Wedding at Cana' (1563)*

Egyptian and Classical antiquities and Italian sculpture

At this point head upstairs to the ground and first floors of the Sully Wing, home to Egyptian and Greek antiquities. The showpiece here, in room 16, is the 2nd-century BC *Venus de Milo*.

For Etruscan and Roman antiquities, make your way to the ground floor of the Denon wing. This is also the showcase for later Italian sculpture, including Michelangelo's *Dying Slave* and Canova's neoclassical *Psyche and Cupid*.

French sculpture

For French sculpture, aim for the Richelieu Wing, where such works as Guillaume Coustou's *Marly Horses* are displayed on the lower ground floor. On the ground floor, the French sculpture collection continues, with works spanning the 5th to 19th centuries. Also located here are Mesopotamian finds such as the black basalt Babylonian Code of Hammurabi (1792–1750 BC), which is one of the world's first legal documents.

French masterpieces

The first floor exhibits some of the Western world's most iconic images. In the Denon Wing are some spectacular large-format French paintings, notably Eugène Delacroix's *Liberty Leading the People*, Théodore Géricault's *Raft of the Medusa* and Jacques-Louis David's *Consecration of Napoleon*. This last picture shows the scene in Notre-Dame at which Napoleon is said to have snubbed the Pope and crowned himself emperor, before crowning Josephine too. There are good views of the roof of the new Department of Islamic Art from the Salle des Etats.

Mona Lisa

Adjacent in Room 6 is Leonardo da Vinci's enigmatic Florentine noblewoman, the *Mona Lisa* (entitled *La Joconde* in French, after the name of her husband: Francesco del Giocondo). This 16th-century portrait was bought into France by François I, when the artist came to work at his court; in the 1980s it was attacked and is therefore now protected by bullet-proof glass. It was also

The *Venus de Milo*

With her serene gaze, soft curves and naturalistic drapery, the *Venus de Milo* was discovered, minus her arms, on the island of Milos in 1820 and promptly purchased by the French government for 6,000 francs. The sensuous statue has been identified as Aphrodite, the Greek goddess of love and beauty, who is often represented half naked, and was probably inspired by the works of Praxiteles. Working in the mid-4th century BC, the Greek sculptor was a forerunner of Hellenistic art, and his nude interpretations of gods and goddesses were often copied.

The ever-popular Mona Lisa

famously stolen by an Italian patriot in 1911, but was thankfully returned in 1914. Hanging alongside is Paolo Veronese's *Wedding at Cana*, where Jesus is said to have turned water into wine.

Other first-floor highlights

At the staircase dividing the Denon and Sully wings is the *Winged Victory of Samothrace* (2nd century BC), a Hellenistic figurehead commemorating a victory at sea, and the glittering Galerie d'Apollon (Apollo's Gallery),

which holds the crown jewels. Note also the gallery's elaborate ceiling by Eugène Delacroix. The first floor of the Richelieu Wing contains Napoleon III's apartments, which now display works of the decorative arts.

French and Dutch painting

The whole of the second floor is devoted to painting, with highlights including Dürer's *Self-Portrait*, Vermeer's *The Lacemaker*, Watteau's *Pierrot* and Ingres' *The Turkish Bath*. Look out for the Rubens Room, devoted to the 24 pictures produced between 1622 and 1625 for Marie de Médicis, illustrating the principal events in her life.

The Richelieu Wing houses works from Flanders, Holland/The Netherlands and Germany (14th to 17th centuries), while the second floor of Sully is devoted to French paintings of the 17th, 18th and 19th centuries.

Other museums

In a separate wing of the Louvre (entrance at 107 rue de Rivoli, www.madparis.fr; Tue–Wed and Fri–Sun 11am–6pm, Thur until 9pm) are other collections, covering the decorative arts, fashion and textiles, and advertising. The **Musée des Arts Décoratifs** presents a survey of interior design from medieval tapestries to 21st-century design. It also contains the **Musée de la Mode et du Textile**, covering Paris fashions and textiles from the 16th century to the

The lost palace

In between the Louvre and the Tuileries Garden was once another palace. Originally built by Catherine de Médicis in the 1560s, it was later occupied by Louis XIV while he waited for Versailles to be built. In the Revolution, however, Louis XVI and Marie Antoinette were forced back to the Tuileries from Versailles and held under house arrest there. The palace was stormed and looted by the mob, leaving over 1,000 corpses strewn around the complex; the king and queen took refuge with the Legislative Assembly. The palace was attacked twice more by revolutionaries, in 1830 and 1848, only to be restored, and then finally burned in 1871 during the Paris Commune, as a symbol of the former royal and imperial regimes.

Palatial decor   *The beautifully landscaped Tuileries*

present, as well as the **Musée de la Publicité**, which exhibits advertising paraphernalia from the Middle Ages to the present day.

Break for lunch

At this point, you'll probably be firmly in need of refreshment. Options in the vicinity of the Louvre include **Chez la Vieille – Adrienne**, see ❹; **La Dame de Pic**, see ❺; **L'Ardoise**, see ❻; **Le Rubis**, see ❼; **La Cordonnerie**, see ❽; and the **Bar de l'Entracte**, see ❾.

The Tuileries

Once sated, head directly west of the pyramid for a stroll round the **Jardin des Tuileries** ❷ (rue de Rivoli, 1st; www.parisinfo.com; daily last Sun of Sept– last Sat of Mar 7.30am–7.30pm, last Sun of Mar–last Sat of Sept 7am–9pm, June–Aug 7am–11pm; free). Once a rubbish tip and clay quarry for tiles (*tuiles*, hence the name), the garden was created in 1564 for Catherine de Médicis in front of what was then the Palais des Tuileries (see box page 34). The Italian-style garden was intended to remind her of her native Tuscany.

Public park

In 1664, Louis XIV's landscape gardener, André Le Nôtre, redesigned the park with his predilection for straight lines and clipped trees. It was opened to the public and became the first fashionable outdoor area in which to see and be seen, prompting the addi-

tion of the first deckchairs and public toilets.

In the 1990s the gardens were renovated, reinstating Le Nôtre's original design and incorporating a new sloping terrace and enclosed garden. The Passerelle Léopold-Sédar-Senghor, a footbridge across the Seine opened in 1999, links the southwestern corner of the gardens to the Left Bank.

Arc de Triomphe du Carrousel

Approaching the gardens from the Louvre, you pass through the **Arc de Triomphe du Carrousel** ❸, which is the smallest of the three arches on the Royal Axis. Erected in 1808 by Napoleon to commemorate his Austrian victories, the pink arch is a rather garish imitation of the triumphal arches built by the Romans, and the four galloping horses on top are copies of four gilded bronze horses, stolen by Napoleon from St Mark's Square in Venice to decorate this memorial. After the emperor's downfall in 1815, the originals were returned.

Sculpture garden

In front of the arch, where the Tuileries Palace once stood, is a group of sculptures of sensuous nudes, created between 1900 and 1938 by Aristide Maillol to adorn the ornamental pools. Numerous other sculptures decorate the gardens, including works by Marly, Le Paultre and Coustou, who were among the first artists to work in

Sitting by the hexagonal pool

the Louvre after Louis XIV abandoned it for Versailles. There are also works by much later artists, including Rodin, Jean Dubuffet, Ellsworth Kelly and David Smith.

Hexagonal pool

At this point continue westwards along the Terrasse du Bord de l'Eau, where Napoleon's children played under the watchful gaze of their father, to the **hexagonal pool** – still a favourite spot for children with boats. There are usually plenty of chairs around here, if you are in need of a rest and even a snooze.

THE ORANGERIE

In the southwest corner of the Tuileries is the **Musée de l'Orangerie ❹** (www.musee-orangerie.fr; Wed–Mon 9am–6pm).

Waterlilies

The building was constructed as a hothouse by Napoleon III, but since the 1920s has been the showcase for eight massive canvases of waterlilies, *Les Nymphéas,* by Claude Monet. In these works, the Impressionist painter captured the play of light and colour on the pond in his garden at Giverny (see page 98) at different times of day, and in doing so caught a dream-like feeling of infinite space. Extensively renovated and reopened in 2006, the two elegant oval rooms

upstairs display the paintings as originally prescribed by Monet himself.

Basement gallery

In the gallery space downstairs is the **Jean Walter and Paul Guillaume Collection**, with high-quality examples of the work of Cézanne, Renoir, Matisse, Picasso, Soutine, Modigliani, Utrillo, Henri Rousseau and others.

JEU DE PAUME

With place de la Concorde on your left, walk to the **Jeu de Paume ❺**, in the northwest corner of the Tuileries. The building was originally constructed in 1861 to house real-tennis courts (hence the name, which means real tennis in French), though it soon became an art museum. From 1940 to 1944 the Jeu de Paume was used to store artworks stolen from French Jews by the Nazi regime. The museum's curator, Rose Valland, a member of the Résistance, notified her fellow *résistants* about which trains contained France's art treasures, so they would not blow them up.

Centre National de la Photographie

The building now houses the stylish **Centre National de la Photographie** (www.jeudepaume.org; Tue 11am–9pm, Wed–Sun until 7pm), which puts on exhibitions of all photographic disciplines, including major fashion retrospectives and contemporary video installations.

Monet's 'Waterlilies' in the Orangerie

Food and drink

❶ CAFÉ MARLY

93 rue de Rivoli, cour Napoléon du Louvre, 1st; tel: 01 49 26 06 60; www.cafe-marly.com; daily 8am–2am; €€€€

Open all day every day and particularly good for breakfast. Sit on the terrace overlooking the glass pyramid or enjoy the plush interior. Kitchen typically open until midnight.

❷ LE FUMOIR

6 rue de l'Amiral-de-Coligny, 1st; tel: 01 42 92 00 24; www.lefumoir.com; daily 11am–2am; €€€

This 'smoking room' feels more like a club than a bar. Regulars sit in squishy leather seats while sipping Mojitos and perusing something from the 3,000-plus library.

❸ LE GARDE-ROBE

41 rue de l'Arbre Sec, 1st; tel: 01 49 26 90 60; Mon–Fri noon–1am, Sat dinner only, closed Sun; €–€€

The 'wardrobe' is a tiny bar with two acclaimed sommeliers, Nathalie and Robin. There are around 200 different wines here, most of which are available by the glass. Food is available in the form of platters of cheese, charcuterie or oysters.

❹ CHEZ LA VIEILLE – ADRIENNE

1 rue Bailleul, 1st; tel: 01 42 60 15 78; www. chezlavieille.fr; Tue-Sat noon–2pm and 6pm–10.30pm; €€€

Classic bistro with good food in homely portions. The Corsican owner will eulogise about his tripe, *pot-au-feu* and his various desserts.

❺ LA DAME DE PIC

20 rue du Louvre, 1st; tel: 01 42 60 40 40; www.anne-sophie-pic.com; daily noon–2pm, 7.30–9.30pm; €€€€

This is the first Paris restaurant of Anne-Sophie Pic, the only female French chef with three Michelin stars. A big fan of aromas and Japanese cuisine, the lunch menu includes crunchy smoked eel, smoked beef chuck with marrow and vegetables with juniper.

❻ L'ARDOISE

28 rue du Mont Thabor, 1st; tel: 01 42 96 28 18; closed Sun lunch; €€€

Excellent food from chef Pierre Jay. Unlike many bistros it opens on Sunday evening.

❼ LE RUBIS

10 rue du Marché-St-Honoré, 1st; tel: 01 42 61 03 34; Mon–Fri 7am–2am, Sat from 9am, closed Sun; €

Wine bar (with rustic *plats du jour* such as sausages with lentils) and an authentic Parisian bistro with lunch and dinner options.

❽ LA CORDONNERIE

20 rue St-Roch, 1st; tel: 01 42 60 17 42; www. restaurantlacordonnerie.fr; closed Sat–Sun; €€€

A small, family-run, nose to tail restaurant serving traditional French classics.

❾ BAR DE L'ENTRACTE

47 rue de Montpensier, 1st; tel: 01 42 97 57 76; Mon–Sat 10am–1am, Sun noon–8pm; €

In an otherwise chic area, this tiny bar has shabby appeal and serves simple snacks.

The iconic Eiffel Tower

THE 7TH

The 7th arrondissement has some of the city's grandest monuments set amongst wide avenues, lofty mansions, ministries and embassies. Most impressive of all is that most iconic of Parisian – and French – symbols: the Eiffel Tower.

> **DISTANCE:** 4.5km (2.75 miles)
> **TIME:** A full day
> **START:** Tour Eiffel (Eiffel Tower)
> **END:** Musée d'Orsay
> **POINTS TO NOTE:** Consider doing this tour on a Thursday, when the Musée d'Orsay has a late closing time of 9.45pm. At the start, expect queues at the Eiffel Tower, which is always busy.

Whichever direction you approach it from, you can't miss the **Tour Eiffel** ❶ (Eiffel Tower; Champs de Mars; www.toureiffel.paris/fr; daily Sept–Apr 9.30am–11.45pm for lifts, 9.30am–6.30pm steps only, late Apr–May 9.30am–12.45am for lifts and steps, Jun–Aug 9am–12.45am for lifts and steps, last lift ascends, at least, 45 minutes prior to closing). At 300m (985ft), the tower is still the city's tallest structure and the world's most visited paid monument.

History

The tower was built according to plans by architect Gustave Eiffel between 28 January 1887 and 31 March 1889 for the Paris Universal Exhibition of 1889 and was intended to stand for only 20 years. Initially, the reception to the tower was frosty, but the advent of radio and the tower's usefulness as a site for antennae secured its future. Even so, it survived a lightning strike in 1902, being 'sold' twice for scrap by a con artist in 1925, a demolition order from Hitler as the Allies neared Paris in 1944, and the ravages of corrosion: tons of rust were removed during its 100th birthday facelift.

First and second platforms

The first platform is 57m (187ft) up, while the second level is at 115m (377ft). In total, there are 1,652 steps. The standard way to ascend is either on foot or in the glass-walled elevators, for which there are always long queues. The first floor has undergone a facelift, including the installation of glass flooring and balustrades (gulp!) and a new state-of-the-art museum on the history of the tower.

One way of avoiding the queues is to go for a meal at one of the tower's two restaurants: **58 Tour Eiffel**, on the first

View from underneath ...*and from the top*

level, and the gourmet **Jules Verne**, which reopened in 2019 after a refurbishment (booking essential for the Jules Verne, recommended for 58; www.restaurants-toureiffel.com), on the second platform, for which there is a private elevator. Of course, if you are not ready for a full meal, you can grab a quick snack at the **macaroon bar** on the second floor.

Third platform

From the second platform, the only way up is by elevator, which means further queuing. This takes visitors to the third level, 300m (985ft) up, from which there are views for approximately 65km (40 miles) on a clear day. The platform on the third level is glazed, and there are signs indicating which sights are which. Also on this level is Gustave Eiffel's office, modelled as it would have been in his day, and the rather more recent addition of a **champagne bar** (10.15am–10.15pm).

Although the tower has restaurants, the **Café Constant**, see ❶, in a nearby street below, is a great option for lunch.

QUAI BRANLY

After lunch, you can visit one of the newest additions to the city's museum collection, the **Musée du Quai Branly – Jacques Chirac** ❷ (37 quai Branly; www.quaibranly.fr; Tue, Wed, Sun 11am–7pm, Thur–Sat 11am–9pm). To reach it, head east from the Eiffel Tower. The anthropology museum opens a window on to cultures as diverse as those of the Pacific Islands and Africa.

CHAMPS DE MARS

Now returning to the Eiffel Tower, walk up through the **Champs de Mars** ❸. Once a military parade ground, it stretches away from the river, ironically, via the glass Wall for Peace, up to the **École Militaire**, France's officer-training academy. Napoleon famously graduated from here in just one year instead of two. Turn left on avenue de la Motte Picquet to place de l'École Militaire, then take the 45-degree turn on to avenue de Tourville, where the **Hôtel des Invalides** ❹ is on your left at place Vauban.

LES INVALIDES

The building of a home and hospital for aged and wounded soldiers was initiated by Louis XIV in 1670 using Libéral Bruant, and later Hardouin Mansart, as architects. It once housed 6,000 invalids. Now, part is still a hospital; the rest a museum of military history.

There is also a chapel for the veterans and a separate royal chapel, the **Église du Dôme** (129 rue de Grenelle, 7th; www.musee-armee.fr; daily Nov–Mar 10am–5pm, Apr–Oct 10am–6pm, also Apr–Sept Tue until 9pm, July–Aug dome open until 7pm), with a gilded dome guarding Napoleon's lavish tomb.

The **Musée de l'Armée** (details same as for the Église du Dôme) comprises

Musée Rodin's exquisite garden

the royal armoury (from which, in 1789, revolutionaries commandeered 30,000 rifles for storming the Bastille), a fine collection of paintings (note Ingres' *Emperor Napoleon on the Throne*), and sections on the two world wars.

MUSÉE RODIN

As you leave Les Invalides turn left on boulevard des Invalides, cross over and then turn right at rue de Varenne. On your right is the **Musée Rodin** 5 (77 rue de Varenne; www.musee-rodin.fr; Tue–Sun 10am–6.30pm).

The museum is housed in the Hôtel de Biron, built in 1728. Rodin moved here in 1908 and struck a deal with the government to bequeath all his works to the state on condition that they would be exhibited in the house and park.

Highlights

As you approach the house, you will find Rodin's famous statue, *The Thinker*, set high up amongst the greenery. Once inside, the decor is bare but elegant. As well as Rodin's works on display here, there are also paintings by Van Gogh, Monet and Renoir, and sculptures by Camille Claudel, Rodin's assistant and mistress. The beautiful gardens behind the house are populated with more of Rodin's statues, and there is also a

Musée d'Orsay

Musée du Quai Branly – Jacques Chirac

café. The museum reopened in 2015 with a brand new layout and new rooms evoking Rodin's life here.

MUSÉE D'ORSAY

Continue down rue de Varenne then turn left at rue de Bellechasse. If you overshoot the turning, on your right on rue de Varenne is the **Hôtel Matignon**, the residence of the French prime minister. Following rue de Bellechasse to the river, you come to the **Musée d'Orsay ❻** (1 rue de la Légion d'Honneur; quai Anatole France; www.musee-orsay.fr; Tue–Sun 9.30am–6pm, Thur until 9.45pm).

This art museum was originally a railway station, built for the Universal Exhibition of 1900. It was subsequently used as a prisoner of war depot during World War II, a set for several films, and then an auction house, before finally becoming a museum in the 1980s.

Exhibits

Dedicated to art from 1848 to 1914, the galleries are organised roughly chronologically. On the ground floor, where trains from southwest France once puffed in, you are taken from Delacroix and Corot up to the birth of Impressionism with early Monet and Renoir. On the mezzanine floor are sections on Art Nouveau design, paintings by neo and Post-Impressionists including Van Gogh, and sculpture by Maillol and Rodin. There is also a restaurant with an exuberant Belle Époque interior. On the top level, which is often crowded, are the Impressionists, notably Manet, Monet, Degas, Renoir, and Cézanne. Check out the views over the Seine from the terrace.

Food and drink

❶ LE CAFÉ CONSTANT

139 rue St-Dominique, 7th; tel: 01 47 53 73 34; daily; €€€

At this fashionable café-bistro, with a zinc bar and blackboard menu, chef Christian Constant produces traditional dishes in modern style.

The imposing Arc de Triomphe

CHAMPS-ÉLYSÉES AND GRANDS BOULEVARDS

This route covers some of the city's smartest avenues, squares and shops, and some big, bold attractions: from the monumental Arc de Triomphe to the Belle Époque Grand and Petit Palais, and the capital's historic department stores.

DISTANCE: 4.75km (3 miles)
TIME: A full day
START: Arc de Triomphe
END: Palais Royal
POINTS TO NOTE: This is a fairly long route, so consider taking the green no. 73 bus down the Champs-Élysées after visiting the Arc de Triomphe. Book in advance for the Grand Palais to avoid the queues.

There is a lot to take in on this route, so you might consider doing it in two halves: the Arc de Triomphe to place de la Concorde, and the Madeleine to the Palais Royal.

ARC DE TRIOMPHE

At metro Charles-de-Gaulle-Étoile, take the subway to access the centre of the roundabout, amidst a chaotic whirl of cars (prangs here are specifically excluded from most insurance policies). In the middle is the **Arc de Triomphe ❶** (place Charles-de-Gaulle; www.paris-arc-de-triomphe.fr; daily Oct–Dec and Jan–Mar 10am–10.30pm,

Apr–Sept 10am–11pm; lift for disabled visitors), begun by Napoleon in 1806 but not completed until 30 years later under King Louis Philippe.

It commemorates Napoleon's army and is decorated with reliefs of famous victories. On the right (with your back to the Champs-Élysées) is the *Marseillaise*, sculpted by François Rude and representing 'Nation' leading the French into combat for the country's freedom. Under the arch is the **Tomb of the Unknown Soldier**, sited here in 1920 and with a flame of remembrance kept constantly alight.

From the top of the monument you can enjoy a spectacular view of the 12 avenues that radiate from l'Étoile ('the star'), as the square is generally known. It was the 'other' Napoleon (Bonaparte's nephew), who, together with the Prefect of Paris, Baron Haussmann, created these wide boulevards flanked by chestnut trees.

CHAMPS-ÉLYSÉES

First initiated by Louis XVI in 1667, the **Champs-Élysées**, or 'Elysian Fields' were laid out by landscape architect

Louis Vuitton's flagship store on the Champs

André Le Nôtre as an extension of the Jardin des Tuileries, running west from the Louvre. During the Second Empire (1852–70) the avenue gave way to sumptuous hotels, chic shops and desirable corporate addresses. In 1871, Bismark's Prussian troops marched up here in triumph, and in 1940 Hitler's did likewise. Today, however, the avenue is home to cinemas, restaurants and the swanky flagship stores of large chains.

Between the top end of the avenue and the **Rond-Point** ❷ at the halfway stage, you pass the high-class **Four Seasons Hotel George V** on the avenue of the same name on your right and the Guerlain perfume store, with its opulent interior, on your left at no. 68. The first right turn off the Rond-Point is **avenue Montaigne**, where many leading fashion houses, including Céline, Chanel, Christian Dior and Prada have flagship stores.

After the Rond-Point, on your right (before the Grand and Petit Palais) is the **Théâtre du Rond-Point**, with its stylish interior (and bar). Meanwhile, on your left is the **Palais de l'Élysée**, the president's residence, down avenue de Marigny. **Ladurée**, see ❶, is worth a stop for cake-tastic refreshments.

If you're feeling up to it and want to visit a charming little museum, take a slight detour off our route, walk all the way up avenue Franklin-Roosevelt until you reach boulevard Haussmann. At No. 158, the **Musée Jacquemart-André** (www.musee-jacquemart-andre.com; daily 10am–6pm) houses a collection of art and furniture that once belonged to wealthy collector Edouard André and his wife, erstwhile portrait painter, Nélie Jacquemart. Highlights include works by Boucher, Rembrandt and Titian, as well as a wonderfully sumptuous dining room (11.45am–5.30pm, from 11am on weekends) with a trompe l'oeil ceiling by Tiepolo, vast windows and delicious cakes.

GRAND AND PETIT PALAIS

The Grand and Petit Palais were built for the World Fair in 1900. The **Grand Palais** ❸ (3 avenue du Général Eisenhower, 8th; www.grandpalais.fr; daily except Tue 10am–8pm, Wed until 10pm; will be closed for renovation from end 2020 to spring 2023), with its 5,000 sq m (54,000 sq ft) of space, hosts blockbuster art exhibitions and the annual Paris Motor Show. There is a cool restaurant, **Mini Palais**, see page 117, which is a good stop for lunch.

The Rococo-style **Petit Palais** ❹ (avenue Winston Churchill, 8th; www.petit palais.paris.fr; Tue–Sun 10am–6pm, Fri until 9pm for special exhibitions) houses the collection of the **Musée des Beaux-Arts de la Ville de Paris**. The building, inspired by the Grand Trianon at Versailles (see page 94), with its polychrome marble, magnificent long gallery and arcaded garden, houses the municipal fine and decorative arts collection, including Greek and Roman antiquities, icons, paintings as well as Art Nouveau furniture.

The famous Ladurée macaroons

PALAIS DE LA DÉCOUVERTE

Behind the Grand Palais on avenue Franklin D. Roosevelt is the **Palais de la Découverte** ❺ (www.palais-decouverte.fr; Tue–Sat 9.30am–6pm, Sun 10am–7pm), a science museum that is particularly fun for children. It is arranged as a series of interactive experiments, with highlights including a planetarium, electrostatics room and an area explaining acoustics.

Both the Grand Palais and the Palais de la Découverte will be closed from 2020–2024 for renovations and upgrades. During the renovations, a 'Grand Palais éphémère' will be built on the Champ de Mars. Both are expected to reopen before the Olympic Games in 2024.

PLACE DE LE CONCORDE

Now proceeding to the bottom of the Champs-Élysées, you enter **place de la Concorde** ❻, flanked by copies of Guillaume Coustou's *Marly Horses* (the originals are in the Louvre). In the centre of this grand square is an **obelisk** from the tomb of Ramses III in Luxor. It was a gift from the Viceroy of Egypt in 1829 and took four years to get here. Previously, this spot had been occupied by the guillotine, and it was here that Louis XVI was beheaded in January 1793.

On the west side of the square is the **Jardin des Tuileries** (see page 35), whereas on the north side are two identical palaces, designed in 1753 by Louis

XV's architect, Ange-Jacques Gabriel. The right-hand one houses the naval ministry; the other is the **Hôtel de Crillon** (at the time of writing it was closed for renovation). The latter was where Marie Antoinette came for piano lessons, where the American delegation to the Paris Peace Conference stayed in 1919, and where the German high command ensconced itself in World War II. Next door is the **Hôtel de la Marine**, an 18th-century palace commissioned by Louis XV, and later used by the Naval Ministry from the Revolution until 2015. It will open its doors to the public for the first time in spring 2020.

Walk up rue Royale between the two palaces. On the wall of no. 4 is an odd-

The Madeleine   *Ornate doorway at the Grand Palais*

ity: a mobilisation notice, now framed, from the start of World War I.

THE MADELEINE

Before long, rue Royale opens out into **place de la Madeleine**, dominated by the neoclassical **Église de la Madeleine** ❼ (daily 9.30am–7pm; free). The church is the fruit of 80 years of anguished debate and false starts – the site was mooted for a stock exchange, public ballroom, library and railway station – until 1806, when Napoleon ordered that a temple to his army be built by Barthélemy Vignon. It took until 1842 for it to be finished, by which time it was decided to consecrate it as a church. Today, it is noted for having one of the finest pipe organs in the city. There are free music recitals in the church every Sunday at 4pm.

Outside, the square offers a flower market as well as the main branches of France's best-known delicatessens, **Fauchon** and **Hédiard**, and the showroom of **Maille**, the mustard makers.

GRANDS BOULEVARDS

Beyond the Madeleine, walk up rue Tronchet then turn right on to boulevard Haussmann, home to the city's most famous department stores, **Au Printemps** ❽ at no. 64, and, nearby at no. 40, **Galeries Lafayette** ❾, both as noteworthy for their architecture as their vast stock.

Fashion emporium Galeries Lafayette

At place Diaghilev turn right down rue Scribe. On this road are the 1862 **Grand Hôtel** and the **Musée de la Parfumerie Fragonard** (9 rue Scribe; www.fragonard. com; Mon–Sat 9am–6pm, Sun until 5pm; free), which focuses on the art of perfume-making.

OPÉRA

Now turn left on to rue Auber to arrive at place de l'Opéra, where the **Palais Garnier** ❿ (www.operadeparis.fr; daily 10am–4.30pm, summer times vary) puts on opera and ballet alongside the newer Opéra Bastille (see page 57). It takes its name from its architect, Charles Garnier, who in 1860 was commissioned by Napoleon III to build an opera house reflecting the pomp and opulence of the Second Empire. The auditorium, decked out in velvet and gilt, is dominated by a vast chandelier, which once crashed down on the audience in 1896. The ceiling was painted by Marc Chagall in 1964. A visit also takes in a library and museum, displaying scores, costumes and sets.

PLACE VENDÔME

As you leave place de l'Opéra, take rue de la Paix, which leads southwest at the bottom of the square. Its exclusive jewellers give a hint as to why it is the most expensive street in the French Monopoly board game.

At its end, you reach the elegant **place Vendôme** ⓫. The square's centrepiece was originally an equestrian statue of Louis XIV, erected in 1699. This was destroyed during the Revolution and then replaced by Napoleon with the **Vendôme Column**, modelled on Trajan's Column in Rome and made from 1,250 cannons captured from the Austrians and Russians. This in turn was pulled down during the 1871 Commune, only to be rebuilt later.

All the same, the square has survived revolution and insurrection remarkably well. Today it is home to wealthy bankers, the salons of haute-couture designers, top jewellers and the newly renovated Ritz hotel, forever linked with Coco Chanel and Princess Diana, who spent her last evening here before her fateful car journey in 1997.

ST-ROCH

At the southern end of place Vendôme, turn left on to rue St-Honoré. Before long, on your left at no. 296, is the late Baroque church of **St-Roch** ⓬ (daily 8.30am–7pm; free). Begun in the 1650s by architect Jacques Lemercier, who also worked on the Louvre, it contains the funerary monuments of landscape designer André Le Nôtre, the playwright Corneille and encyclopaedist Diderot. On the church's exterior are pockmarks from musket shot after Napoleon's troops put down a Royalist revolt here in 1795.

COMÉDIE-FRANÇAISE

Continue to place André-Malraux, home to the French national theatre, the **Comédie-Française** ⓭ (closed for 6 months from

Jewellers line Place Vendôme

Buren's columns at the Palais Royal

spring 2020; entrance on place Colette; tel: 01 44 58 15 15; www.comedie-fran caise.fr). Most productions are of the classical repertoire, by playwrights including Molière, Racine and Corneille.

PALAIS ROYAL

On the far side of the theatre is the **Palais Royal** . The palace's main courtyard, which is entered through the archway, contains 250 black-and-white striped columns, erected by artist Daniel Buren in 1986. Beyond are elegant gardens (daily dawn–dusk; free) enclosed by a three-storey peristyle erected in 1780 to house cafés, shops and apartments, and, with its rents, to replenish the coffers of its owners, the Orléans family, after a century of profligate spending. The passageways are enjoying a regeneration sparked by the opening of fashion designer Stella McCartney's store here.

Built for Cardinal Richelieu, and subsequently the childhood home of Louis XIV, the palace passed into the hands of the dukes of Orléans in the early 1700s. They turned it into a den of gambling and prostitution and forbade the police entrance. It was a focal point for intrigue during the Revolution, and afterwards, once restored to the Orléans, as iniquitous as before. Wellington supposedly lost so much money in its casinos that Parisians claimed they had recouped the cost of their war reparations. Today, it is a tamer place, housing the Ministry of Culture and Constitutional Council.

Slip out of the northern end of the Palais Royal's gardens and cross the tiny rue des Petits-Champs. To your left are **Galerie Vivienne** and **Galerie Colbert**, beautifully preserved skylit passages with mosaic floors and brass lamps, and both lined with shops.

At this, the route's end, you can rejoin the metro just south of the Palais Royal or, to the north, visit **Willi's Wine Bar**, see ②, for a drink.

Food and drink

① LADURÉE

75 av. des Champs-Élysées, 8th; tel: 01 40 75 08 75; www.laduree.fr; Mon–Fri 7.30am–11pm, Sat until midnight, Sun until 10pm; €€–€€€

This Parisian 'lab' of master macaroon-makers produces tiptop macaroons every day and develops new flavours. At this branch you can also enjoy breakfast or a full meal of French classics at the restaurant amid Louis XIV-style decor. Other branches include 16 rue Royale (also on this walk).

② WILLI'S WINE BAR

13 rue des Petits-Champs, 1st; tel: 01 42 61 05 09; www.williswinebar.com; Mon–Sat noon–12am, closed Sun; €€€

As well as dozens of wines from around the world sold by the glass or bottle, this bar serves a variety of traditional, seasonal French dishes along with simpler offerings such as *croques* and platters of charcuterie.

Centre Pompidou's 'inside-out' architecture

BEAUBOURG AND LES HALLES

This compact area is really in the thick of things, historically, artistically and commercially. Whereas once the city's food markets drew the crowds, today, the attractions are modern art, historic monuments and upmarket food shops.

DISTANCE: 2.5km (1.5 miles)
TIME: Half a day
START: Centre Pompidou
END: Rue de Rivoli
POINTS TO NOTE: Allow at least a couple of hours in the Centre Pompidou – longer, if you are particularly keen on modern and contemporary art.

This route starts at the front of the Centre Pompidou, where the sloping cobbled terrace acts as a stage for a variety of street performers.

CENTRE POMPIDOU

The **Centre Pompidou** ❶ (place Georges Pompidou; www.centrepompidou.fr; daily 11am–10pm, Thur until 11pm, closed on Tue; tickets until 9pm), or 'Beaubourg,' as it is known locally, after the street that runs behind it, continues where the Musée d'Orsay (see page 41) leaves off, with art from 1905 onwards.

The architecture

The building was completed in 1977 on the designs of architects Renzo Piano and Richard Rogers. The museum is now so popular that it is hard to appreciate the initial storm of criticism regarding its 'inside-out' architecture (blue units transport air conditioning, green ones are water circulation, red tubes are transport routes, and yellow ones indicate electric circuits).

Entrance and services

Inside, on the ground floor, there is a complete posting of the centre's events and exhibits. No matter when you visit, you are likely to find a free exhibition in the massive entrance hall. On the ground floor, there is a shop selling a selection of works by modern designers. While on the first floor, there is a public library and a cinema in addition to the Mezzanine Café. Flammarion bookshops can be found on several floors.

The permanent collection

A selection from the permanent art collection of over 100,000 works is on levels 4 and 5. Parts are rehung every year. The period from 1905 to the 1960s is dealt with on level 5, with works by artists such as Kandinsky, Klee, Klein, Matisse, Picasso and Pollock, and sections on Dadaism and Surrealism. Art from the 1960s to the present day is on level 4 and includes works by Andy Warhol, Verner Panton, Joseph Beuys, Jean Dubuffet and Anselm Kiefer.

Studio Brancusi, IRCAM and Stravinsky Fountain

In front of the Pompidou is a pavilion containing the studio (Wed–Mon 2–6pm; included in main ticket) of Romanian-born sculptor, Constantin Brancusi (1876–1957). The artist lived in this studio for 30 years, bequeathing it to the French state on his death. It has been set up here just as he left it.

Next to the Pompidou, and part of the same organisation, is the Institute of Research and Co-ordination into Acoustics and Music (IRCAM), on place Igor Stravinsky. This centre, created by composer Pierre Boulez, hosts concerts of avant-garde music.

Between the Centre Pompidou and the church of St-Merri, the **Stravinsky Fountain** is a colourful fountain with grotesque creatures and contraptions spouting water. It was created by artists Niki de Saint-Phalle and Jean Tinguely as a homage to composer Igor Stravinsky's *Firebird* ballet.

La Canopée, the symbol of a rejuvenated Forum des Halles

ST-MERRI

Beyond the Stravinsky Fountain, on the south side of the square is the Gothic church of **St-Merri** ❷ (76 rue de la Verrerie; daily Apr–Sept 3–7pm, Nov–Mar 2–6pm; free). It dates mostly from the 16th century, but its bell has been tolling since 1331, which makes it the oldest in Paris. There are music recitals at 8pm on Saturdays and 4pm on Sundays.

RED LIGHTS

Exiting the church on rue St-Martin, turn right, up towards the Pompidou, and then left at rue Aubry le Boucher. Go straight on, across the busy boulevard de Sébastopol and on to rue Berger. At the corner of rue St-Denis, take a good look up and down. Rue St-Denis is the city's main red-light district. The area in which you stand is rather tame, though things do become more overt a little further along.

LES HALLES

Rue Berger now opens out into place Joachim du Bellay. The Fontaine des Innocents, the Renaissance fountain in the middle, was moved here from the nearby Cimetière des Innocents, which was demolished in 1786.

Leaving the place by rue Pierre-Lescot on your right, you come to **Les Halles** ❸. The name refers to the covered food market that was established here by King Philippe Auguste in 1183. In the 1850s,

huge glass-and-iron buildings were erected, and Emile Zola later wrote a novel, *The Belly of Paris* (1873), set around the area. Sadly, in 1971 the structure was demolished in the interests of safety and urban renewal, and the markets moved to the southern suburb of Rungis. The Forum des Halles shopping centre and transport intersection that replaced it was largely a place to avoid – so no-one wept its demolition in 2010. It has now been replaced by a shiny new shopping and entertainment complex complete with a new, undulating roof, **La Canopée**, and vast garden landscaped into various themed areas.

TOUR JEAN SANS PEUR

Past Les Halles, turn left on to rue Rambuteau and right on to rue Montorgueil. Where rue Étienne-Marcel, now one of the city's most fashionable shopping streets, crosses rue Montorgueil, turn right for the **Tour Jean Sans Peur** ❹ (20 rue Étienne-Marcel; www.tourjeansanspeursite. wordpress.com; Wed–Sun 1.30–6pm), a fortified town house built 1409–11 by Jean, Duke of Burgundy.

The duke acquired his nickname, meaning 'John the Fearless', from military exploits in Bulgaria against the Turks. On return to Paris, he assassinated his rival, Louis d'Orléans, and sparked the Hundred Years' War between the Armagnac and Burgundian factions. Jean fled, but returned two years later and, necessarily security conscious, added the tower to his mansion.

Église St-Eustache

ST-EUSTACHE

Retracing your way back down rue Montorgueil, perhaps stopping en route at **Stohrer**, see , take the narrow passage de la Reine de Hongrie on your right, then continue over to the Impasse St-Eustache, which leads to the church of **St-Eustache** ❺ (2 impasse St-Eustache; Mon–Fri 9.30am–7pm, Sat 10am–7.15pm, Sun 9am–7.15pm; free). Built from 1532 to 1640, it has a Gothic exterior and fine Renaissance interior. Its 8,000-pipe organ is highly renowned: Berlioz and Liszt played here in the 19th century, and recitals are still held weekly, at 5.30pm on Sundays.

Around Place René-Cassin
Emerging from the other (south) side of the church, you find yourself on place René-Cassin with its massive sculpture by Henri de Miller of a giant head and cupped hand, entitled *Écoute* (Listen). Continue west on rue Coquillière. A curiosity on your right is **E. Dehillerin**, purveyors of pots and pans to Paris's chefs.

BOURSE DE COMMERCE

The rotunda on your left is the **Bourse de Commerce** ❻ (2 rue de Viarmes). The Bourse was built in 1767, on the site of Marie de Médicis' palace, and functioned as the city's grain market. Until recently, it housed the Chamber of Commerce but in late 2019 it will become the home of the **Collection Pinault – Paris**, a showcase of French billionaire François Pinault's contemporary art collection.

ASTROLOGER'S COLUMN

As you leave the Bourse, turn left and go round the back to find the **Colonne Médicis** ❼. The plaque at its base states that the pillar is the sole relic of the manor house built in 1572 by Catherine de Médicis (wife of Henri II) for her astrologer, Cosimo Ruggieri, who, with his patron, regularly climbed up the 31m (102ft) -high tower's spiral staircase to read the future in the stars. Unfortunately, you can no longer go inside.

FONTAINE DU TRAHOIR

Head down rue Sauval, turn left at rue St-Honoré and then immediately right on to rue de l'Arbre-Sec. On the street corner is the **Fontaine du Trahoir** ❽, a fountain rebuilt by Soufflot in 1776 and dripping with stone icicles. Follow the road to rue de Rivoli and turn right to rejoin the metro at Louvre-Rivoli.

MARAIS AND BASTILLE

Among the most vibrant areas of town, the Marais and the Bastille are an unlikely but successful blend of ingredients: aristocratic mansions, the centre of the LGBTQ scene, the home of the Jewish community and the epicentre of Parisian nightlife.

DISTANCE: 4.5km (2.75 miles)
TIME: A full day
START: Hôtel de Ville
END: Place de la Bastille
POINTS TO NOTE: It is not intended that you visit every museum. There is, however, the opportunity to combine a stroll in the historic streets with some shopping, lunch, a museum tour and finally a rest in a park or café.

The area covered in the first part of this tour was once a swamp – '*marais*' is French for 'marsh'. It was drained in the 16th century and developed as an aristocratic residential district, until, with the rise of Versailles, it fell into neglect. Largely untouched by town planner Baron Haussmann in the 19th century, it fell into further decline, until by the 1960s it was derelict and rat infested. Due to be cleared, it was saved by Culture Minister André Malraux, who safeguarded many of the buildings and initiated the restoration. Today it is a fashion-

able quarter full of boutiques, galleries, bars and restaurants.

HÔTEL DE VILLE

Begin at the **Hôtel de Ville ❶** (29 rue de Rivoli; http://en.parisinfo.com; only guided tours, once or twice a week, to be booked in advance tel: 01 42 76 54 04; closed on Sun; free), since 1357 the seat of local government in Paris. The building is a recreation of the original structure, commissioned by François I in 1533 and gutted by fire during the Paris Commune of 1871.

It has been the scene of many historical events, including the proclamation of the Third Republic in 1870 and Charles de Gaulle's famous speech to the assembled crowds on 25 August 1944 during the Liberation of Paris.

Its most notable features are the extravagant Salle des Fêtes (ballroom), a magnificent staircase and some opulent chandeliers. On the north side, on rue de Rivoli, is an

The Hôtel de Ville

entrance to an exhibition with information about the city.

THE MARAIS

Head north from the pedestrianised square in front of the Hôtel de Ville where, in medieval times, hangings and other gruesome executions took place. Cross the rue de Rivoli, walk up rue du Temple and turn right at rue Sainte-Croix-de-la-Bretonnerie, the hub of the LGBTQ scene. Turn left off this road on to rue des Archives, and then continue until you reach rue des Francs-Bourgeois.

Hôtel de Soubise and Hôtel de Rohan

At no. 60, in the **Hôtel de Soubise ❷**, is one of three sites in France housing the French National Archives (Mon, Wed–Fri 10am–5.30pm, Sat–Sun 2–5.30pm), opened by Napoleon in 1808 and containing documents from the Merovingians to the Ancien Régime. Around the corner at 87 rue Vieille-du-Temple is the **Hôtel de Rohan ❸**, which hosts exhibitions relating to French history and has a lovely Jardin de Rohan which is accessible to the public (free).

If for nothing else, it is worth a visit for the magnificent buildings themselves, which were home to the Guise family from 1553; it is probably from here that the Catholic League planned the St Bartholomew's Day Massacre. In 1700, the Duke de Rohan, Prince of Soubise, bought the estate and revamped it, with Rococo interiors decorated by Boucher, Lemoine and van Loo.

Lunch options and shopping

While on rue Vieille du Temple, there are several good options for lunch, including **Le Petit Fer à Cheval**, see ❶. Back on rue des Francs-Bourgeois there are designer boutiques and cafés, too. The Marais is one of the few Paris districts in which a large number of shops open for business on a Sunday, its busiest and most crowded day of the week.

When sated, continue a little further to find rue Elzévir on your left.

Musée Cognacq-Jay

The outside of the 1580s mansion at no. 8 rue Elzévir is understated, but inside is the exquisite fine and decorative art collection of Ernest Cognacq, who founded La Samaritaine department store in 1870, and his wife Marie-Louise Jay, in the **Musée Cognacq-Jay ❹** (www.museecognacqjay.paris.fr; Tue–Sun 10am–6pm; free).

Here, 18th-century refinement is embodied in salons and 'cabinets' with the feel of a private house. On the panelled walls are paintings and drawings by Chardin, Nattier, Fragonard, Watteau, Reynolds, Guardi and Canaletto. Displayed on delicate furniture and in cabinets are Meissen por-

Musée Picasso exhibition

celain figures by master modeller J.J. Kändler.

Musée National Picasso

Up the road on rue de Thorigny is the **Musée National Picasso ❺** (5 rue de Thorigny, www.museepicassoparis. fr; Tue–Fri 10.30am–6pm, Sat–Sun and holidays 9.30am–6pm). The museum is housed in the Hôtel Salé, so-called because its 17th-century owner grew rich through collecting taxes on salt. Over 5,000 paintings, sculptures, collages, drawings and other works of art in the collection were given to the state on the artist's death. Another 1,000 works were later bought by the museum. Not all are by Picasso: his personal collection includes works by Cézanne, Matisse (his great rival), Modigliani and Braque. The revamped museum spreads out onto three floors: the first floor displays all Picasso's periods, in chronological order; the second floor hosts temporary exhibitions and the third floor holds a library and archives.

Hôtel Carnavalet

Nearby is the **Musée de l'Histoire de Paris** (Hôtel Carnavalet, 23 rue de Sévigné; www.carnavalet.paris.fr), the city's historical museum, which will re-open at the end of 2019 after an extensive renovation. Housed within two adjoining 16th- to 17th-century mansions, it tells the story of Paris from Roman times to the present using paintings, memorabilia and historic interiors.

Jewish Quarter

Past the Carnavalet, take rue Pavée opposite to reach the Jewish Quarter also known as 'Pletzl', which is Yiddish for 'little place'. Off to the right on rue des Rosiers are several Jewish bakeries and restaurants, including the excellent **L'As du Fallafel**, see ❷, a legacy of Sephardic immigration after the French withdrawal from its colonial territories in North Africa.

At 10 rue Pavée is the extraordinary **Synagogue ❻** (tel: 01 48 87 21 54;

The Jewish Quarter

Hôtel Salé, home to the Musée Picasso

10am–5pm; visits by request only; free). It is architecturally notable for its 1913 Art Nouveau facade by Hector Guimard, who also designed the furnishings inside. The building was severely damaged by a bomb (along with six other Parisian synagogues) during anti-Semitic demonstrations on the evening of Yom Kippur 1941. It was restored and is now a national monument. A few minutes' walk west of here is the **Mémorial de la Shoah** (17 rue Geoffroy l'Asnier, 4th; www.memorialdelashoah.org; Sun–Fri 10am–6pm, Thur until 10pm, closed Jewish holidays; free) which is

the most important centre in Europe devoted to the Holocaust and has a permanent exhibition on the concentration camps.

Retrace your steps and continue along rue Pavée and turn left onto rue de Rivoli, which soon becomes rue St-Antoine.

Hôtel de Sully

At no. 62, enter the large wooden doors of the **Hôtel de Sully** **❼** (www. hotel-de-sully.fr; courtyards open daily 9am–7pm; free). This impressive 17th-century mansion, built to plans by architect Jean Androuet du Cerceau

The delightful place des Vosges

in 1625 and then bought in 1635 by Sully (Finance Minister under Henri IV), is the HQ of Monuments Nationaux, the organisation that looks after France's most important historical buildings.

Walk through the cobbled courtyard, and on into the pristine gardens.

Place des Vosges

A gate in the far corner provides an escape on to **place des Vosges** . Built from 1605 to 1612 by Henri IV, this large, elegant square was originally called place Royale, but was renamed in tribute to the first French *département* (county) to pay its war taxes to the Republican government. Famous past residents have included Madame de Sévigné, salon hostess and letter writer, at no. 1bis (born here in 1626), poet Théophile Gautier and writer Alphonse Daudet at no. 8, and Cardinal Richelieu at no. 21. Upmarket pâtissier **Carette**, see ③, has a tea room here which is a good spot for a pit stop.

Maison de Victor Hugo

Located in the southeast corner of the square, at no. 6, is the **Maison de Victor Hugo** ❾ (www.maisonsvic torhugo.paris.fr; closed until March 2020), erstwhile home of the author of *Les Misérables* and *The Hunchback of Notre-Dame*. Hugo lived here from 1832 to 1848, until Napoleon III's coup d'état forced him, as a staunch republican, into 20 years of exile on Guernsey. Inside, you can see his rooms, some

furnished with a few of his own pieces – he was an expert, though eccentric, carpenter – as well as a number of his drawings and first editions.

BASTILLE

Leaving place des Vosges and the Marais behind, walk down rue de Birague and turn left at rue St-Antoine.

Place de la Bastille

The vast **place de la Bastille** ❿ takes its name from the notorious prison stormed by revolutionaries on 14 July 1789. On its capture, only seven prisoners remained inside, but the rebels did find it a useful supply of arms and gunpowder. The Banque de France office now stands on its site.

In the centre of the square is the **Colonne de Juillet** (July Column), which was erected in the 19th century to honour vic-

Le Petit Fer à Cheval

Opéra Bastille

tims of the 1830 and 1848 revolutions. The golden statue at the top, the *Génie de la Bastille*, is a representation of Liberty.

Opéra National de la Bastille

On the southeast side is the **Opéra National de la Bastille** ⓫ (120 rue de Lyon; www.operadeparis.fr; tours Sept–mid-July). One of Mitterrand's *grands projets* (see page 31), it was constructed in 1989 to designs by Canadian-based Uruguayan Carlos Ott, but has since been plagued with criticism: for its acoustics, its vast cost and the poor quality of its architecture. Netting has already been put up to stop its granite slabs falling down.

The fashionable east

If you take rue de la Roquette off place de la Bastille and turn right on to rue de Lappe, you find yourself on a street lined with bars, nightclubs, cafés and boutiques, a reflection of the area's fashionable status, which boomed in the 1990s. (Nowadays, it's still trendy, although not quite as cutting edge as it once was). The area's fashion credentials are also reflected in its peppering with contemporary galleries. At the end of rue de Lappe, if you turn left on to rue de Charonne, you will find where the Lavignes Bastille gallery (est.1973), at no. 27, used to be. This was one of the best-known in the neighbourhood (Andy Warhol exhibited here). For more contemporary art, the open galleries can be found further up on your left on rue Keller. To return to Bastille, retrace your steps or turn left at the northern end of rue Keller on to rue de la Roquette.

Food and drink

❶ LE PETIT FER À CHEVAL

30 rue Vieille du Temple, 4th; tel: 01 42 72 47 47; daily 9am–2am; €€
Cramped but fun café-bistro with a horseshoe-shaped bar out front and small box of a dining room with old metro benches at the back. A case-study in artful insouciance.

❷ L'AS DU FALLAFEL

34 rue des Rosiers, 4th; tel: 01 48 87 63 60; www.l-as-du-fallafel.zenchef.com; Mon–Thur, Sun noon–11pm, Fri noon–4pm, Sat 6.30pm–11pm; €
The place for falafel. Try the special (vegetarian) sandwich: garlicky falafel, hummus, fried aubergine, red cabbage, salted cucumber and harissa. Lamb shawarmas are also recommended. Hectic but fun ambience. Takeaway also available.

❸ CARETTE

25 place des Vosges, 4th; tel: 01 48 87 94 07; www.carette-paris.fr; daily 7.30am–midnight; €
Smart tearoom for light savoury snacks and mouth-watering cakes and desserts.

Much-loved Shakespeare & Co

THE LATIN QUARTER

This university area takes you from Roman remains to medieval theological colleges, to Enlightenment seats of learning, to the student riots of 1968. And the tradition continues today, with students and academics smoking outside the libraries, drinking in the cafés and browsing in the bookshops.

DISTANCE: 3km (2 miles)
TIME: A full day
START: Jardin des Plantes
END: Place St-Michel
POINT TO NOTE: The first part of the route is good for children, who will love the Jardin des Plantes.

The route begins across the road from the Gare d'Austerlitz, on place Valhubert, at the entrance to the **Jardin des Plantes ❶** (Botanical Gardens; daily 7.30am–8pm, 8am–5.30pm in winter; free).

JARDIN DES PLANTES

The gardens were established by Louis XIII's physician in 1626 as a source of medicinal herbs and opened to the public in 1640 as the 'Jardin du Roi'. In the 1700s, a maze, amphitheatre and several museums were added.

On your left as you enter is the first of these museums, that of palaeontology and comparative anatomy, the **Galerie de Paléontologie et d'Anatomie com-** parée (Wed–Mon 10am–6pm), displaying fossils, skeletons and shells. Outside are huge replica dinosaurs.

Museum of Mineralogy and Geology

Now make your way to the statue of the zoologist Jean-Baptiste Lamarck, and from here walk up the avenue of plane trees to the statue of an illustrious former keeper of the gardens, Georges-Louis Leclerc, Count de Buffon. En route, you pass the rose garden in front of the newly renovated **Galerie de Minéralogie et de Géologie** (Museum of Mineralogy and Geology; Wed–Mon 10am–6pm, Oct–Mar until 5pm), which contains meteorites, minerals, jewels and giant crystals.

The Zoo

On the opposite side, is the **Ménagerie** (Mon–Sat 9am–6pm, Sun until 6.30pm, winter hours vary). This zoo was established during the Revolution with animals from royal and aristocratic collections.

Beyond the statue of de Buffon is the **Grande Galerie de l'Évolution** (Wed–Mon 10am–6pm), opened in 1889 to display part of the collection of 7 million

Mosquée de Paris courtyard

skeletons, insects, and stuffed birds and mammals. Most are now in an underground research centre, but following renovation, the exhibition space shows some 7,000 choice specimens, including 257 endangered or extinct species.

MOSQUÉE DE PARIS

Leaving the gardens by the gate on rue Geoffroy St-Hilaire, cross over towards the corner of rue Daubenton and the **Mosquée de Paris** ❷ (Paris Mosque; 2bis place du Puits de l'Ermite; tours daily 9am–noon and 2–6pm, summer hours vary). This Hispano-Moorish-style complex was built in 1922 to commemorate North African participation in World War I. It incorporates a museum of Muslim art, a Moroccan-style market, a pretty **tearoom**, see ❶, and a Turkish bath.

ARÈNES DE LUTÈCE

Turn left out of the tearoom and continue walking north along rue Geoffroy St-Hilaire. Go straight on at the crossroads, as the road becomes rue Linné. Take a left into rue des Arènes. On your right is the entrance to the **Arènes de Lutèce** ❸ (daily 8am or 9am–6/7.30pm or 8pm depending on the season; free). This Roman amphitheatre was rediscovered in the 1860s during the construction of the nearby rue Monge. Where gladiators once

Panthéon fresco

fought before an audience of 15,000, Parisians of all ages now play boules.

RUE MOUFFETARD

As you leave, turn right and climb the few steps to rue Rollin. At the end of this road, turn left on to rue du Cardinal-Lemoine. You soon come to **place de la Contrescarpe**, with its pleasant **Café Delmas**, see ②.

On the far side of the square is **rue Mouffetard** ④, once a Roman road, now famous for its food market (Tue–Sat, all day, and Sun am).

TOWARDS THE PANTHÉON

Retrace your steps to place de la Contrescarpe, then keep going, along rue Descartes, into the heart of the Latin Quarter. This university area derives its name from the fact that Latin was widely spoken here

Medieval tapestry

The Musée de Cluny's tapestry series *The Lady and the Unicorn* is one of the greatest works of art of the Middle Ages in Europe. It depicts the five senses plus a sixth, mysterious, sense. In this last scene, the lady puts into her jewel-case the collar that she was wearing in the other five. Above her is the inscription, 'To My Only Desire'. The most popular theory is that this signifies the refusal of temptation, and the renunciation of the five senses, previously stated.

in the Middle Ages. Turn left at rue Clovis, to see, on your left, the **Lycée Henri IV**, one of France's most elite secondary schools, and, on your right, the church of **St-Étienne-du-Mont** ❺ (place Ste-Geneviève; Mon 6.30–7.30pm, Tue–Fri 8.45am–7.45pm, Wed till 10pm, Sat 8.45am–noon and 2–7.45pm, Sun 8.45am–12.15pm and 2.30–7.45pm; free). Along with St Geneviève, the patron saint of Paris, are buried playwright Jean Racine and the scientist and philosopher Blaise Pascal.

The Panthéon

Coming out into the vast place du Panthéon, the neoclassical **Panthéon** ❻ (www.pantheonparis.com; daily 10am–6pm, Apr–Sep until 6.30pm) looms up before you. It was designed by Soufflot as a church to St Geneviève for Louis XV, who wanted to give thanks for his recovery from illness. After the Revolution it became a Temple to Reason and the burial place of the nation's great minds, including Voltaire, Rousseau, Hugo, Zola, and Pierre and Marie Curie. Another highlight is a 67m (220ft) replica of Foucault's pendulum (an experiment to show the rotation of the earth).

THE SORBONNE

Next take rue Cujas off the square to your right, turn right on to rue St-Jacques and head down the hill. The **Sorbonne** ❼, one of the oldest colleges (1253) of the university of Paris, is on your left. The buildings date mainly from the late 19th century, although the domed chapel, in

Cluny's 'The Lady and the Unicorn'

which Cardinal Richelieu is buried, is 17th century. At the bottom of the hill on your right is the Collège de France, founded in 1530 as a humanist alternative to the decidedly Catholic Sorbonne.

MUSÉE DE CLUNY

Turn left on to rue des Écoles then turn right at the square Paul-Painlevé for the **Musée de Cluny – Musée National du Moyen-Âge** ❽ (Wed–Mon 9.15am–5.45pm). Once the residence of the Abbots of Cluny, this is the only surviving Gothic residence in Paris. It also incorporates the remains of a huge Gallo-Roman bathhouse complex, built *c.*200 AD.

On display in the main museum are medieval manuscripts, textiles (notably the *Lady and the Unicorn* tapestries – see box), stained glass and sculpture, including 21 of the original heads of the kings of Judah, crafted in 1220 for the front of Notre-Dame.

TOWARDS THE SEINE

After the museum, return to rue St-Jacques and continue downhill, bearing right on to rue Dante. A little further on is **square René Viviani**, on the far side of which is the 12th-century church of **St-Julien-le-Pauvre** ❾, originally a sanctuary for pilgrims on their way to Santiago de Compostela.

Taking rue St-Julien towards the river you reach famous English-language bookshop **Shakespeare & Co.** (www.shakespeare andcompany.com; Mon–Sat 10am–10pm, Sun 12.30–8pm), on the left. On the pavement by the river are *bouquinistes* (riverside bookstalls) and if you look east, you'll see the striking **Institut du Monde Arabe** ❿ (1 rue des Fossés-St-Bernard, 5th; closed Mon). Designed by Jean Nouvel, the glass-and-steel nine-storey structure houses a cultural centre and museum of Islamic art. Views from the rooftop restaurant are stunning.

Walking west, cross rue St-Jacques and go down **rue de la Huchette**. There are tourist traps on this medieval street, but look out for **rue du Chat-Qui-Pêche**, the city's narrowest street on the right. You emerge on place St-Michel with its **fountain** of St Michael slaying a dragon.

Legendary café Les Deux Magots

ST-GERMAIN

With its elegant streets and squares, St–Germain is a magnet for designer fashion shops, chic cafés and restaurants. But before the glossy present was a more rumbustious past: revolutionaries plotted, actors drank, and Hemingway stole pigeons from the Jardin du Luxembourg to cook and eat.

DISTANCE: 3km (2 miles)
TIME: A full day
START: Place St-Michel
END: Jardin du Luxembourg
POINT TO NOTE: End your walk with a picnic in the Jardin du Luxembourg.

The route begins at **place St-Michel ❶**, from where you should head west on to rue St-André-des-Arts, into a warren of streets full of shops, bars and restaurants. Turn left on to rue de l'Éperon, right on to rue du Jardinet, then continue to cour de Rohan.

HISTORIC QUARTER

You finally emerge onto the **cour du Commerce St-André ❷**, where you should turn left. During the Revolution, Danton lived at no. 1 on this cobbled passage and, in the courtyard of no. 9, Dr Guillotin was testing his gruesome invention on sheep.

Le Procope
On a tiny road parallel, look out for **Le Procope** (13 rue de l'Ancienne-Comédie; daily noon–midnight, Thur, Fri, Sat until 1am), supposedly the oldest surviving café in Paris. It started out as a coffee house in 1686, and playwrights Racine and Molière were reportedly regular customers here.

BOULEVARD ST-GERMAIN

Exiting the passage, turn right on to boulevard St-Germain. You soon come to place St-Germain-des-Prés, where one of the city's oldest churches is situated, as well as two famous café-restaurants: the **Café de Flore**, see ❶, and **Les Deux Magots**, see ❷.

St-Germain-des-Prés
The church of **St-Germain-des-Prés ❸** (Tue–Sat 8.30am–8pm, Sun–Mon 9am–8pm; free) takes its name from an 8th-century cardinal of Paris, who was buried in the 6th-century abbey of Ste-Croix-St-Vincent on this site.

The present church was built in the 11th and 12th centuries and was once part of a vast monastery, suppressed

St-Germain chapel

during the Revolution. The church survived and is the only Romanesque one left in Paris. In the 19th century it was converted into a saltpetre factory and then underwent several less-than-sensitive restorations. Inside, the 17th-century philosopher René Descartes' ashes are interred under the window in the second chapel.

Outside, in square Laurent-Prache, are relics of a magnificent chapel built in 1255. Look out for Pablo Picasso's portrait bust of the poet Guillaume Apollinaire (1880–1918).

From the square, turn right on rue de l'Abbaye, then left on to the pretty rue de Furstemberg.

MUSÉE DELACROIX

The **Musée National Eugène Delacroix** ❹ (www.musee-delacroix. fr; Wed–Mon 9.30am–5.30pm), at nearby 6 place de Furstemberg, comprises the 19th-century painter's former home, studio and garden. The artist moved here in 1857 to be near St-Sulpice, where he had been commissioned to paint several murals. He died in the bedroom in 1863. While the Louvre and Musée d'Orsay

house his major Romantic paintings, here you can see smaller works and sketches.

TOWARDS ST-SULPICE

Back on rue de Furstemberg, continue as far as rue Jacob and turn left. At no. 56, peace documents recognising the independence of the United States of America were signed by Benjamin Franklin and David Hartley, King George III's representative in France.

Detail inside St–Sulpice

Retracing your steps, now turn left (north) on rue Bonaparte. On your right by the river is the **Institut de France**, housing the Académie Française, whose membership of 40 'immortels' are responsible for the official dictionary of the French language. Back on rue Bonaparte, walk all the way down (south) past a succession of stylish shops. Eventually, you arrive at place St-Sulpice and its lion-flanked Fontaine des Quatre-Évêques. This chic square is used every summer for antiques and poetry fairs.

Montparnasse

On the south side of the Jardin du Luxembourg is boulevard du Montparnasse. In the early 20th century, the area became a magnet for artists and composers including Chagall, Picasso and Stravinsky. The atelier where Russian artist Marie Vassilieff ran an art academy and canteen and threw exotic parties is now art centre Villa Vassilieff (21 avenue du Maine; www.villavassilieff.net; Tue–Sat 11am–7pm; free) while the former studio of Modernist painter and sculptor Antoine Bourdelle is now the Musée Bourdelle (18 rue Antoine Bourdelle, www.bourdelle.paris.fr; Tue–Sun 10am–6pm; free). Today the area is best known for the 59-storey Tour Montparnasse (www.tourmontparnasse56.com), which has viewing platforms and a restaurant, Le Ciel de Paris, on the 56th floor. Note that the tower will close in late 2020 for a total transformation in time for the Olympics.

ST-SULPICE

The eastern side of place St-Sulpice is dominated by the vast Italianate church of **St-Sulpice** ❺ (daily 7.30am–7.30pm; free). Begun in 1646 to a design by Jean-Baptiste Servandoni, the church took a further five architects and 120 years to complete. The result is ponderous: the towers, one of which is higher than the other (unfinished), have been likened to 'municipal inkwells'. The church has many historical links, though: the Marquis de Sade was baptised here, Victor Hugo was married here, and it featured in Prévost's 18th-century novel *Manon Lescaut*.

Highlights

Inside, the first chapel on the right (Chapelle de Sainte Agnès) was decorated by Eugène Delacroix. In the nave are two great conch shells presented to François I by the Republic of Venice. Note also the fine organ with 6,700 pipes and check the noticeboard for details of concerts held in the church.

In the left wing of the transept is a gnomon, a white marble obelisk with a line of copper leading away from it in the floor, representing the Paris meridian. It was completed in 1727, and improved in 1744. When the sun shines through the 'eye', located 25m (82ft) above the ground in a transept window facing south, the device is meant to indicate the 'true' midday hour and the approximate date.

St-Germain chic   *The delightful Jardin du Luxembourg*

ODÉON

Leaving the church, walk along rue St-Sulpice and turn left at rue de Condé to reach the **carrefour de l'Odéon**. Next turn right up rue de l'Odéon, an enclave for publishers and antiquarian bookshops for at least 150 years. At no. 12 Sylvia Beach and the original Shakespeare & Co. bookshop (see page 61) first published James Joyce's *Ulysses*.

At the top of the road is the grand neo-classical **Théâtre de l'Odéon** ❻, built from 1779 to 1782. It was here that Beaumarchais's *Marriage of Figaro* was first performed in 1784 and the actress Sarah Bernhardt gave many of her finest performances.

Beyond the theatre is rue de Vaugirard, where a pit stop at the engaging **Au Petit Suisse**, see ❸, may well be required, before then finishing the route in the Jardin du Luxembourg.

JARDIN DU LUXEMBOURG

At the entrance to the **Jardin du Luxembourg** ❼ (daily dawn–dusk; free) is the **Palais du Luxembourg**, built in the 1620s for Marie de Médicis, widow of Henri IV, by Salomon de Brosse. Its Italianate style was supposed to remind Marie of the Pitti Palace in her native Florence. It now houses the Senate. Next door, at 19 rue de Vaugirard, is the **Musée National du Luxembourg** ❽ (www.museeduluxembourg.fr; daily 10.30am–7pm, Mon until 10pm),

France's oldest public art gallery (1750).

Inside the gardens are statues, fountains, a boating lake, cafés, a playground, a puppet theatre, a merry-go-round, boules pitches, deckchairs, orchards with 300 varieties of apple, and an apiary, where you can take courses in beekeeping.

Food and drink

❶ CAFÉ DE FLORE

172 boulevard St-Germain, 6th; tel: 01 45 48 55 26; www.cafedeflore.fr; daily 7.30am–1.30am; €€€
Grand, historic café with Art Deco interior. In the days when it was less expensive, it was frequented by Jean-Paul Sartre and Simone de Beauvoir.

❷ LES DEUX MAGOTS

6 place St-Germain-des-Prés, 6th; tel: 01 45 48 55 25; www.lesdeuxmagots.fr; daily 7.30am–1am; €€€
Rival to Café de Flore, and also once habituated by Sartre and de Beauvoir, as well as Hemingway, Picasso and Gide, among others. Like many places that have become an institution, it is also now pretty expensive and can get very busy. Light food.

❸ AU PETIT SUISSE

16 rue de Vaugirard, 6th; tel: 01 43 26 03 81; www.aupetitsuisse.fr; Mon–Fri 6.30am–2am, Sat–Sun from 7.30 €
Unpretentious café with terrace. Snacks served noon till closing time.

Art Nouveau Abbesses metro station

MONTMARTRE

Romantic relic of a simpler, more vital world, or clichéd victim of its own success? Approach Montmartre with a fresh mind and steer clear of the obvious tourist traps, and you will find plenty here to engage and surprise.

> **DISTANCE:** 3.5km (2.25 miles)
> **TIME:** A full day
> **START:** Les Abbesses
> **END:** Place de Clichy
> **POINT TO NOTE:** Montmartre's streets are very steep, so this is not the best route if you prefer easy walks on the flat. (Taking the funicular up the hill will take some strain out of the climb.)

Montmartre has always stood slightly apart from the rest of the city. For much of the 19th century it was mined for gypsum and still retained a country charm with its vineyards, cornfields, flocks of sheep and 40 windmills. The lofty isolation of the hill and its cheap lodgings attracted artists and writers. Painters and their models frequented place Pigalle, and people flocked to the Moulin Rouge. Impressionism, Fauvism and Cubism were conceived in the area's garrets, bars and dance halls.

LES ABBESSES

At the exit of metro Les Abbesses, note the Art Nouveau canopy by Hector Guimard, one of only two (the other is at place Dauphine) in the city to survive. Opposite is another Art Nouveau structure: **St-Jean de Montmartre ❶**. Built 1897–1904 to designs by Anatole de Baudot, the church is an early example of construction with reinforced cement and brick. Inside are several wall paintings (unfinished) executed at the end of World War I and depicting the Gospel of St-John.

Now, making a mental note that nearby is **Rose Bakery**, see ❶, a good lunch option for later, head east off the square on rue Yvonne Le Tac. At no. 11 is the **Chapelle des Martyrs ❷**, where, according to legend, St Denis, the first Bishop of Paris, picked up his head after being decapitated by the Romans in AD 287. He is then said to have walked off with it to where the basilica of St-Denis now stands 10km (6 miles) to the north. Montmartre means 'hill of the martyr'.

PLACE ST-PIERRE

The road now becomes rue Tardieu and then place St-Pierre. With Montmar-

The Sacré-Cœur   *Capturing the view from La Butte*

tre's white basilica rising above you, walk to the far side of the place, where, on your left, is the **Halle St-Pierre**. This 19th-century covered market hall designed by Victor Baltard houses the **Musée de la Halle St-Pierre ❸** (Mon–Fri 11am–6pm, Sat until 7pm, Sun noon–6pm, closed in Aug), which shows brut and naïve artworks by artists from around the world. It also hosts music concerts and lectures, and has an excellent bookshop.

Now either walk up through square Willette, laid out in terraces in 1929, or take the funicular railway (the fare is one metro ticket) to reach the terrace in front of Sacré-Cœur.

SACRÉ-CŒUR

Sacré-Cœur ❹ (35 rue Chevalier-de-la-Barre; www.sacre-coeur-montmartre.com; basilica: daily 6am–10.30pm, dome: May–Sept 9.30am–8pm, Oct–Apr 9.30am–5pm, crypt was closed at the time of writing for security reasons; entry to basilica free, charge for dome and crypt) was constructed after the suppression of the 1871 Paris Commune, which had been passionately supported by the

Street artists in Place du Tertre

anarchist Montmartrois. The church was built in appeasement for the bloodshed, and because of this, and its arguably rather mediocre architecture, has never been well-loved by local residents.

Work started on the basilica in 1875 and was not completed until 1914, and it was not consecrated until 1919. The architect, Paul Abadie, based his design on the Romano-Byzantine cathedral of St-Front in Périgueux and used Château-Landon stone, which secretes calcite when it rains, bleaching the walls a bone-white colour.

The dome, up 237 narrow spiral steps, offers a wonderful view over Paris. There is also a huge bell, the Savoyarde, weighing 18 tonnes. From the stained-glass gallery beneath is a good view of the cavernous interior.

PLACE DU TERTRE

Now head west from the church on rue Azais and turn right onto rue St-Eleuthère to arrive at place du Tertre, which regrettably now has more than its fair share of overpriced restaurants and bad would-be artists. Stay briefly on the square, however, for a couple of more worthwhile sights.

St-Pierre-de-Montmartre

On your right is the simple church of **St-Pierre-de-Montmartre** ❺ (daily 9.30am–7pm; free), the second oldest in Paris (after St-Germain-des-Prés), dating from 1133, and all that remains

of the old Abbey of Montmartre. A Benedictine nunnery since the 12th century, the abbey was destroyed during the Revolution. The church itself was abandoned and only re-consecrated in 1908. It is noteworthy too that, according to the earliest biography of St-Ignatius Loyola, it was here that the vows were taken that led to the founding of the Jesuits.

Inside, the walls and columns (Roman in origin) of the nave seem to have bent with age and lean outwards. If you are here on Toussaint (All Saints' Day – 1 November), visit the small, romantic graveyard behind the church, since this is the only day of the year that it is open.

Dalí Museum

On the opposite side of the square is place du Calvaire, which forms a terrace with a fine view over Paris. At its far end, on the corner of rue Poulbot, is the **Espace Dalí** ❻ (11 rue Poulbot; www.daliparis.com; daily 10am–6.30pm, July–Aug until 8.30pm), with more than 300 works by the Surrealist artist.

The original bistro

Following rue Poulbot round, turn right at rue Norvins to reach 6 place du Tertre, home of **La Mère Catherine** ❼, reputedly Paris's first bistro. Originally a drinking den for revolutionaries, the old inn apparently served Russian soldiers during the Allied occupation of 1814. As they ordered their drinks – forbidden

Retro postcards for sale   *On the steps of St-Pierre-de-Montmartre*

by the Russian military authorities – they shouted 'bistro' meaning 'quickly', thereby creating a Parisian institution.

Leaving the crowd of place du Tertre behind, head back to rue Norvins, then off onto rue des Saules where, at no. 22, is legendary cabaret **Au Lapin Agile** (www.au-lapin-agile.com; Tue–Sun 9pm–1am). On wooden benches by scarred tables (though with original paintings by Gill and Léger), you are treated to a glass of cherries in *eau de vie* and a night of songs and poems in the tradition of Aristide Bruant. Once upon a time Renoir and Verlaine laid tables here, and Picasso paid for a day's meals with one of his *Harlequin* paintings: now worth millions of pounds.

Take the second right onto rue Cortot.

MUSÉE DE MONTMARTRE

At 12 rue Cortot, in the oldest house on the Butte, is the **Musée de Montmartre** ❽ (www.museedemontmartre.fr; daily 10am–6pm, Apr–Sept until 7pm), which chronicles the life and times of the artists' quarter.

This manor house was originally the country home of Rosimund, an actor in Molière's theatre company. Two hundred years later and the house had been divided into studios, with Renoir, Dufy, and Utrillo and his mother, Suzanne Valadon, living and working here. (Valadon's lover, the composer Erik Satie, lived in various lodgings on rue Cortot in the 1890s.)

The displays

Today, the lower floors are devoted to the history of Montmartre through revolutions and wars, whereas the upper floors evoke the bohemian artistic life of legend. As well as a reconstruction of Utrillo's favourite café, L'Abreuvoir, there is an artist's studio and artworks by Utrillo, Dufy and Toulouse-Lautrec. The long-neglected studio-apartment of both Valadon and Utrillo was restored in 2014 and is now open to the public. The gardens, where Renoir used to paint, are a peaceful oasis.

VINEYARD

Behind the museum are vineyards that were planted in 1933 in hom-

---

The New Athens

In the mid-19th century, the area south of boulevard de Clichy now known as La Nouvelle Athènes (New Athens) attracted writers, artists, composers, actresses and courtesans. For a sniff of this rarefied past, visit the Musée Gustave Moreau (14 rue de La Rochefoucauld; www.museemoreau.fr; Wed–Mon 10am–6pm) with its lovely double-height studio packed with Symbolist paintings, or the Musée de la Vie Romantique (right) at 16 rue Chaptal (Tue–Sun 10am–6pm) with its memorabilia on the novelist George Sand and her circle of friends, including her lover the composer Chopin.

La Maison Rose, loved by Maurice Utrillo

age to the vines cultivated here since the Middle Ages. In early October, the grape harvest attracts hundreds of volunteers, and processions and parties take place in the neighbouring streets. About 300 litres (634 pints) of wine are sold at auction, with proceeds going to the Montmartre Festival Committee.

CASTLE OF THE MISTS

On the other side of rue des Saules from rue Cortot is rue de l'Abreuvoir, which becomes the allée des Brouillards. Here, **square Suzanne-Buisson** occupies the former gardens of the **Château des Brouillards** ❾, which stands opposite. The house was built in 1772 and takes its name from the windmill that was here before and could only be seen when the fog lifted. Converted outhouses on its grounds were once inhabited by Renoir and the Symbolist poet Gérard de Nerval. Later the château became a dance hall, and then a squat before being restored.

RENOIR'S WINDMILL

Turn south on rue Girardon, then right onto rue Lepic. On your right is the **Moulin de la Galette** ❿. Built in 1604, the windmill became a dance hall in the 19th century and was immortalised by Renoir in his 1866 painting of the same name.

BATEAU-LAVOIR

Now head back to rue Girardon, noting the other windmill here, the Moulin de Radet. Head south along the narrow rue d'Orchampt and continue to its end and place Émile-Goudeau. At no. 13, artists' studios stand in place of the wooden ramshackle building in which Braque and Picasso invented Cubism. **Le Bateau-Lavoir** ⓫, so named because it resembled a floating laundry, was where Picasso painted *Les Demoiselles d'Avignon* (1907), recalling the prostitutes of Barcelona; in rooms alongside, Apollinaire and Max Jacob developed their liberated verse-form. Sadly, the building burnt down in 1970 just as it was about to be renovated.

STUDIO 28

Turn right onto rue Garreau, which soon becomes rue Durantin, and, at the crossroads with rue Tholozé, turn left.

On your left is the famous cinema, **Studio 28** ⓬, where, in 1930, Luis Buñuel's *L'Âge d'Or* (The Golden Age) caused a riot on only its second screening due to its overtly sexual content (the film only got past its censors through its being excused as 'the dream of a mad man'). Members of the fascist League of Patriots threw ink at the screen, attacked members of the audience, and destroyed art work by Dalí, Miró, Man Ray, Yves Tanguy, and others on display in the lobby.

The singer Dalida lived here   *The Moulin Rouge – you can't miss it*

The film was subsequently banned for 50 years.

Rue Lepic

At the end of rue Tholozé, turn right, and soon after join the lower reaches of rue Lepic. No. 54 was home to Vincent Van Gogh and his brother Theo for two years in the late 1880s. At no. 42 is **À la Pomponnette**, see ②, while at no. 15 is **Les Deux Moulins**, where Amélie Poulain waited on tables in the eponymous film. At the bottom of rue Lepic, turn right onto boulevard de Clichy.

PIGALLE

At the bottom of the Butte is **Pigalle**, or 'Pig Alley', as it was known to American soldiers during World War II. Once known exclusively for being the city's seedy red-light district, the area is cleaning up its act and is in parts now edgily cool. Some sex shops and seedy nightspots are still in evidence, but many of the old brothels and erotic cabarets are being replaced by trendy clubs (such as the Divan du Monde at 75 rue des Martyrs), chic boutiques and fashionable bars and restaurants.

The Moulin Rouge

Coming down the boulevard de Clichy, almost immediately on your right is the **Moulin Rouge** ⑱ (82 boulevard de Clichy; www.moulinrouge.fr), where a troupe of scantily clad 'Doriss'

dancers delight spectators with their nightly show.

The club's history is gloriously scandalous. In 1896, the annual Paris Art School Ball was held here and featured the first fully nude striptease, by one of the school's models. She was arrested and imprisoned, and students went to the barricades in the Latin Quarter, proclaiming 'the battle for artistic nudity'.

Sparing a thought for the poet Jacques Prévert, who used to live just next door, now continue down the boulevard de Clichy towards place de Clichy, where a cluster of restaurants offer a gastronomic end to this tour.

Food and drink

① ROSE BAKERY

46 rue des Martyrs, 18th; tel: 01 42 82 12 80; www.rosebakery.fr; daily 9.30am–6.30pm; €–€€

Hip Franco-British café which serves savoury snacks, including quiches and salads, and yummy cakes to eat in or take away. A good option for vegetarians, there is also a branch in the Marais (30 rue Debelleyme, 3rd).

② À LA POMPONNETTE

42 rue Lepic, 18th; tel: 01 46 06 08 36; www.alapomponnette.com; daily lunch and dinner; €€€

Family-run bistro offering excellent renditions of classic French dishes.

Clean lines at Monsieur Bleu

TROCADÉRO

This walk to the Trocadéro in the 16th offers a varied selection of Parisian museums. Art or fashion, Asian antiquities or naval history: choose carefully which ones to visit, since to see them all would be exhausting.

DISTANCE: 1.25km (0.75 mile)
TIME: Half a day
START: Place de l'Alma
END: Palais de Chaillot
POINT TO NOTE: The time above includes the walk and two museum stops.

Start at place de l'Alma, and look out for la Flamme, a counterpart to the flame of the Statue of Liberty (gifted to the US by France). Then head west up avenue du Président Wilson. On your left, at no. 13, is the **Palais de Tokyo** ❶, built, along with the nearby Palais de Chaillot, for the 1937 World Fair and now home to two museums.

The **Musée d'Art Moderne de la Ville de Paris** (www.mam.paris.fr; due to re-open late 2019 following renovations; Tue–Sun 10am–6pm; free except exhibitions), the municipal collection of modern art, is notable for Matisse's *La Danse* (1932) and Raoul Dufy's *Fée de l'Electricité* (Electricity Fairy) mural.

In the opposite wing is the **Site de Création Contemporaine** (www.palaisdetokyo.com; Wed–Mon noon–midnight). Described as a 'laboratory for contemporary art', it focuses on young artists. There is also a fashionable restaurant here, **Monsieur Bleu**, see ❶.

Asian sculptures in Musée Guimet

MUSÉE DE LA MODE

On the other side of the road, in a mansion built by Gustave Eiffel, is the fashion museum, the **Palais Galliera – Musée de la Mode ❷** (10 avenue Pierre-1er-de-Serbie; www.palaisgalliera.paris.fr; closed until January 2020 for expansion works). Drawing on its collection of over 12,000 outfits and 60,000 accessories from the 18th century to the present, exhibitions continue to take place at off-site locales during the renovations (check website).

MUSÉE GUIMET

Continue along avenue du Président Wilson to reach place d'Iéna where, at no. 6, is the **Musée National des Arts Asiatiques – Musée Guimet ❸**, the national museum of Asian art (Wed–Mon 10am–6pm). It was founded in 1889 as a museum of world religions by Émile Guimet, a 19th-century industrialist and traveller. With the addition of the Oriental collections from the Louvre, it now owns 45,000 items. Highlights include Chinese paintings from Dunhuang, the Treasure of Begram from Afghanistan and the Giant's Way, part of the temple complex from Angkor Wat, Cambodia.

PALAIS DE CHAILLOT

Continuing west for a further 5 minutes brings you to place du Trocadéro and the **Palais de Chaillot ❹**. This huge Art Deco complex contains three museums and a theatre.

First on your left, in the east wing, is the **Cité de l'Architecture et du Patrimoine** (www.citechaillot.fr; Mon, Wed, Fri–Sun 11am–7pm, Thur until 9pm) – the world's largest museum of architecture, charting France's architectural history from cathedral portals to Renaissance fountains up to contemporary buildings.

In the west wing is the **Musée National de la Marine** (www.musee-marine.fr; closed until 2021). Displays of cannon barrels, early torpedoes, uniforms and paintings take you from ancient galleons to nuclear submarine. Also here is the **Musée de l'Homme** (www.museedelhomme.fr; Wed–Mon 10am–6pm), an anthropology museum whose star exhibits include the skull of philosopher René Descartes. The revamped museum now boasts a café and a restaurant with views of the Eiffel Tower.

Walk down the steps behind the Palais de Chaillot for superb views of the Tower.

Food and drink

❶ MONSIEUR BLEU

Palais de Tokyo, avenue de New York, 8th; tel: 01 47 20 90 47; www.monsieurbleu.com; daily noon–2am; €€€
Design-conscious and fun, this restaurant has a traditional menu and a terrace with views over the Eiffel Tower. There's also **Les Grands Verres** (tel: 01 85 53 03 61; daily noon–1am) a Parisian pioneer in environmental and culinary sustainability, also with a good cocktail bar.

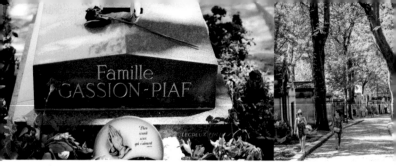

Edith Piaf's resting place

PÈRE LACHAISE

Wander in the maze of celebrity graves at Père Lachaise, then walk through Belleville, which, once a country village, then a workers' district, now offers an understated mix of cafés, artists' collectives, cottages and gardens.

DISTANCE: 4km (2.5 miles)
TIME: Half a day
START: Père Lachaise
END: Place du Colonel Fabien
POINT TO NOTE: The best metro station for the start of this tour is Philippe Auguste.

From metro Philippe Auguste, turn right on to boulevard de Ménilmontant for Paris's smartest address for the dead, the cemetery of **Père Lachaise** ❶ (www.pere-lachaise.com; Nov–mid–Mar 8am–5.30pm, Sat from 8.30am, Sun from 9am, mid–Mar–Oct 8am–6pm, Sat from 8.30am, Sun from 9am; free). 'Residents' include Chopin, Molière and Rossini, as well as more recent luminaries: Edith Piaf, Gertrude Stein, Oscar Wilde, Jim Morrison and Yves Montand. At the main entrance on boulevard de Ménilmontant, visitors can pick up free maps pinpointing the more famous graves.

The cemetery is named after the confessor of Louis XIV, Père La Chaise, who lived in a Jesuit house here. In 1804 it was established as a cemetery by Napoleon, although it was initially deemed too far from the city to attract many burials. As a marketing ploy, the administrators organised the transfer of the remains of writers La Fontaine and Molière, and, later, lovers Héloïse and Abélard.

CEMETERY TOUR

Walk up avenue Principale and turn right on to avenue du Puits to find the tomb of Abélard and Héloïse. In the 12th century, Héloïse was a student of the controversial theologian, Abélard, and secretly became his lover and wife. Her father's fury ended in Abélard being castrated and banished to a monastery, and Héloïse forced into a convent. However, they have left to posterity their letters, professing a pure and faithful love.

Artists and writers

Retrace your steps to avenue Principale and make your way past the graves of Colette, Rossini and Alfred de Musset, up the shady paths to the chapel on the hilltop.

Strolling in Père Lachaise

Statue of a praying girl in Père Lachaise

Continue in the same direction, on avenue des Combattants Étrangers morts pour la France, passing the grave of the spiritualist Allan Kardec and on to the grand crematorium, bordered by the graves of Isadora Duncan, Maria Callas, Max Ophuls and Max Ernst. From here, it is only a short walk to an exit gate or, if you are ready for more, take a right turn along avenue Circulaire to the top (eastern) corner of the cemetery and the Mur des Fédérés.

Mur des Fédérés

This wall was where the last 147 anarchist rebels of the Paris Commune, a courageous uprising against Prussian domination in 1871, were lined up and shot after their final resistance among the graves the night before. The bullet holes are still visible. Also here is the Jardin du Souvenir, home to many monuments commemorating the dead of World War II.

Lunch stop

Leaving the cemetery behind via the exit nearest the crematorium, you emerge on to rue des Rondeaux. Turn left towards Gambetta metro station, left again on to place

Martin Nadaud and then look for **rue Sorbier** where you can lunch at **Le Rez-de-Chaussée**, see ①.

BELLEVILLE

The tour now continues into **Belleville**. In the early 19th century, this was a fertile country village but in the second half it evolved into a poor working-class area and a forge of class agitation. Today the *quartier* is subject to gentrification, com-

Relaxing in the Parc de Belleville

plete with the usual transient symptoms of art collectives and small-scale impromptu galleries.

Passage Plantin

Cross over rue de Ménilmontant on to rue Henri Chevreau, after looking left to take in the view towards the Centre Pompidou. Follow the road as it veers to the left and then turn right at rue des Couronnes, and then left down an alley, **Passage Plantin** ❷, with pretty houses that were typical of Belleville before the property developers moved in.

Parc de Belleville

At the other end of Passage Plantin, turn left on rue du Transvaal, which soon becomes rue Piat. Here, there is a fine view over the **Parc de Belleville** ❸ (8 or 9am–5.45pm in winter, 9.30pm in summer; free) and the wider city. The park cascades down the hillside, and is most attractive in its lowest reaches.

Rue Rébeval

Continue on rue Piat until you reach rue de Belleville. Just before you cross over onto rue Rébeval, look for no. 72, outside which singer Edith Piaf was supposed to have been born under a lamp-post.

On rue Rébeval, watch out for the quirky brick building at Nos 78–80, on the left-hand side. Although now the Paris-Belleville School of Architecture, this was once the Meccano factory and the source of many a child's constructive Christmas presents.

Butte Bergeyre

At this point, turn right on to rue Pradier, then left again on to avenue Simon-Bolivar, which leads to the corner of the **Parc des Buttes-Chaumont** ❹ (see page 80).

Follow the western edge of the park on rue Manin and turn left down avenue Mathurin-Moreau. On the left-hand side is the **Butte Bergeyre** ❺, which before World War I was the site of a fairground. It is now a quaint complex of lanes, houses and gardens clinging to the hillsides.

Place du Colonel-Fabien

Avenue Mathurin-Moreau leads to place du Colonel-Fabien, named after the *nom de guerre* of the French Communist resistance hero, Pierre Georges. Fittingly, the square is now dominated by the headquarters of the French Communist Party in a Modernist building designed by Brazilian architect Oscar Niemeyer.

To return to central Paris, pick up the metro at Colonel-Fabien, nearby.

Food and drink

❶ LE REZ-DE-CHAUSSÉE

10 rue Sorbier, 20th; tel: 01 43 58 30 14; www.restaurant-rdc-paris20eme.com; daily 11am–3pm and 7–11.30pm; €€
Simple French classics are this friendly bistro's best offerings: *oeufs en cocotte*, *faux filet*, *mousse au chocolat*. Great value.

The popular Chez Prune

NORTHEAST PARIS

Catch a boat, cycle or stroll up the canal to an often-overlooked area of Paris that has lots to appeal to both children and adults: a science museum, 3-D cinema, submarine, music museum, beautiful parks and spectacular city views.

> **DISTANCE:** 9km (6.5 miles)
> **TIME:** A full day
> **START:** Place de la Bastille
> **END:** Parc des Buttes-Chaumont
> **POINT TO NOTE:** If you choose to cycle up the canal, you can pick up a Vélib' bike (see page 124) at place de la Bastille or place de la République.

The route begins by following the Canal St-Martin from **place de la Bastille ❶** up to the northeast of Paris. Either start early and board a Canauxrama tour boat (www. canauxrama.com; reservations essential), or cycle or stroll up the canal towpaths.

CANAL CRUISE

If you choose to go by boat, note that cruises run in both directions. The 2.5-hour cruise begins at the **Port de l'Arsenal ❷** (by 50 boulevard de la Bastille, and near the restaurant "Le Grand Bleu" or Bassin de la Villette at No. 1 avenue Jean Jaurès, in front of the Jaurès Café). Departures are at 9.45am and/or 2.30pm daily,

and commentaries are in both English and French. Sit on the top deck for the best views.

Going underground

Napoleon commissioned the canal partly to allow more water into the city centre and earn the citizens' affection.

At place de la Bastille, the canal goes underground, emerging again beyond **place de la République ❸**. As you glide under the city, you pass through a strip of the canal that is lit by pavement gratings that send shafts of light down to the water. The different colours of mortar indicate where restoration work has been carried out; the area overhead has been untouched since the canal was built.

Hôtel du Nord

At **quai de Valmy** and **quai de Jemmapes**, you emerge amid trees and gardens into a unique Parisian landscape, punctuated with 19th-century iron footbridges and locks. On the right bank is the **Hôtel du Nord ❹**, the inspiration for Marcel Carné's 1938 film of the same name, and now an atmospheric bar and bistro. In

The Canal sees a lot of boat traffic

summer, you can enjoy views of the canal from the outside terrace.

Behind it is the **Hôpital St-Louis** ❺, built from 1607 to shelter plague victims. Adjacent, on rue de la Grange-aux-Belles, are two noteworthy *chanson* cafés for evening wine and song, Chez Adel (no. 10) and Apostrophe (no. 23).

Back on quai de Valmy, at no. 200, is one of the city's foremost alternative cultural venues, the **Point Ephémère** (www.pointephemere.org). A 1930s former warehouse, it has been converted into artists' studios, a club, music studios, a gallery and a café. Another lovely café on quai de Valmy is **Chez Prune**, see ❶.

Rotonde de la Villette

Going north, at place de Stalingrad you reach the **Rotonde de la Villette** ❻, one of Claude Nicholas Ledoux's beautifully designed tollhouses (now hosting exhibitions). It marks the start of the **Bassin de la Villette**, built for Napoleon in 1808, and bordered by stylish new cinemas, beautiful old warehouses and some less appealing 1960s and 1970s high-rise blocks. In true post-industrial fashion, some warehouses here have been reclaimed by artists' cooperatives as studio space.

At the top end of the basin is an ingenious piece of 19th-century engineering: a hydraulic lifting bridge, the **Pont de Crimée** ❼, which displaces a whole section of road. Just beyond the port is the Parc de la Villette, where the canal divides into the canals de l'Ourcq and St-Denis, and where the boat ride comes to an end.

PARC DE LA VILLETTE

The **Parc de la Villette** ❽ (avenues Corentin-Cariou and Jean-Jaurès; www.lavillette.com; daily; free) was created in 1986 as one of François Mitterrand's *grands projets* (see page 31), on a 50-ha (136-acre) site, where the city's meat market once stood.

Géode

On the left of the canal is the **Géode** ❾ (www.lageode.fr; Tue–Sun 10.30am–8.30pm), a polished-steel sphere, which looks rather like something from outer space. Inside, the hemispheric theatre has one of the world's largest screens and dizzily slanted seating. Movies are made especially for this huge screen, many on a natural science theme.

Cité des Sciences

The **Cité des Sciences et de l'Industrie** ❿ (www.cite-sciences.fr; Tue–Sat 10am–6pm, Sun 10am–7pm; ground-floor exhibits in main hall free), or science museum, was created from the shell of an unfinished slaughterhouse building.

Inside, there is plenty to see, particularly for children (of all ages): try out the jet-pack simulator for armchair astronauts, experience the sensations of space sickness or weightlessness, practise on a flight simulator, and perform experiments using mirrors, electricity and tricks of perspective. There are other exhibits on the origins of life, the underwater world, plant life, and there are even

Philharmonie concert hall · 'Pocket submarine' at the Cité des Sciences

robotic animals in a cybernetic zoo.

The **Planétarium** runs several programmes a day. There is an extra charge for these: make sure to buy your tickets as soon as you arrive, they sell out quickly.

The **Cité des Enfants** has lots of fun, interactive attractions for children, with areas divided according to age (2–7 and 5–12 year olds).

The park

The park itself is the largest in Paris, spread over more than 55,5ha/136 acres. It was designed by Swiss landscape architect Bernard Tschumi as a collection of gardens, each with a different theme. Children should enjoy the Dragon's Garden, the Garden of the Winds and the Garden of Childhood Fears, with its fairy-tale mystery, dark colours and engaging sound system. Adults may prefer the subtlety of the Garden of Shadows and the beauty of the Garden of Bamboos.

In summer, the Triangle Meadow is a wonderful place to sit and enjoy a picnic. You can even watch an outdoor movie here, on a giant inflatable.

At regular intervals in the park, you will spot bright-red enamelled-steel buildings, which are contemporary versions of 18th-century French architectural fantasies or follies. Each one looks different

The Géode at the Parc de la Villette

and is devoted to a special activity; the Folie Argonaute, for example, leads you to a real submarine that arrived via the Canal de l'Ourcq.

Zénith

Next to the northern bridge is a large, grey, solid-looking tent, the **Zénith**, a concert hall that can seat up to 6,300 people and is best known as the centre of Paris's thriving rap scene. Opposite, a new-wave circus performs below the big top of **Espace Chapiteaux**.

On the east side of the canal is **La Grande Halle**, a fine example of 19th-century iron architecture. Until 1974, it housed France's national meat market, but was rendered obsolete by modern refrigeration and poor design – the cows could not get up the steps – and is now an exhibition space with a hip café-restaurant, **La Petite Halle**, see ②. Shows range from the prestigious, often controversial Paris Biennale contemporary art show to the International Architectural Fair, to fashion shows. Nearby is the **Maison de la Villette**, home to an exhibition on the history of the park.

Philharmonie de Paris

On the extreme southeastern edge of the park is Paris's major new music complex, the **Philharmonie de Paris** (www.philharmoniedeparis.fr). It includes the new **Philharmonie 1** designed by Jean Nouvel, which has a spectacular Grand Hall seating 2,400, as well as **Philharmonie 2**, formerly the Cité de la Musique. The complex houses the **Musée de la Musique** (Tue–Fri noon–6pm, Sat and Sun 10am–6pm), which charts the development of classical, jazz and folk music and holds an impressive collection of more than 7,000 musical instruments.

CIMETIÈRE DE LA VILLETTE

Leaving La Cité de la Musique and Parc de la Villette, cross avenue Jean-Jaurès (perhaps stopping for lunch at the epicure's valhalla, **Au Bœuf Couronné**, see ③). Note that there is a pick-up/drop-off point (station Vélib') for city bikes on Jean-Jaurès at this point.

Head down Sente des Dorées and then take the second right on to rue Manin for the pleasant 15-minute walk to the Parc des Buttes-Chaumont. On the way, a minor detour on to rue d'Hautpoul on your right brings you to the **Cimetière de la Villette** ⓫ (mid-Mar–Oct Mon–Fri 8am–6pm, Sat from 8.30am, Sun from 9am, Nov–mid-Mar Mon–Fri 8am–5.30pm, Sat from 8.30am, Sun from 9am; free). Through a monumental gateway you will find a mini version of Père Lachaise cemetery with huge 19th-century tombs set under a canopy of trees.

PARC DES BUTTES-CHAUMONT

The **Parc des Buttes-Chaumont** ⓬ (daily Oct–Mar 7am–8pm, Apr and Sept 7am–9pm, May–Aug 7am–10pm; free), one of the finest parks in Paris, was built by Baron Haussmann in the 1860s on the

Parc des Buttes–Chaumont   Musée de la Musique guitars

site of a rubbish dump and gypsum quarry. The uneven ground provided a perfect setting for a wooded, rocky terrain, and a lake has been created around an artificial 50m (165ft) 'mountain', which is capped by a Roman-style temple, with a waterfall and a cave containing fake stalactites. Ice-skating and boating are also on offer, and the puppet show or 'Guignols' in the open-air theatre has been a popular attraction for more than 150 years (weather permitting, open-air shows are on Wed, Sat and Sun; during winter months the shows are indoors and heated).

Russian church

On the western side of the park, near where you entered, is the atmospheric Russian church of **St-Serge-de-Radogène** ⑬ (visit by appointment only, minimum 10 people; recommended donation is 4 €). You approach it through a gateway at 93 rue de Crimée. Originally built as a Protestant church in 1861, it was acquired by the Russian Orthodox Church in 1924 to minister to the influx of Russian immigrants fleeing the Revolution.

BACK TO CENTRAL PARIS

To get back into town from here, you can take the metro from Buttes-Chaumont or Botzaris. Alternatively, take bus no. 75, which goes to the Centre Pompidou and Hôtel de Ville. The bus begins back at place de la Porte de Pantin, near where you left the Parc de la Villette, but has various stops at points around Parc des Buttes-Chaumont. It only runs until about 11.50pm.

Food and drink

① CHEZ PRUNE

36 rue Beaurepaire, 10th; tel: 01 42 41 30 47; Mon–Sat 8am–2am, Sun 10am–2am; €
Watch the world go by at this cornerstone of trendy Canal St-Martin. Respectable food at lunch time and tapas-style snacks at night.

② LA PETITE HALLE

211 avenue de Jean-Jaurès, 19th; tel: 9 82 25 91 81; www.lapetitehalle.com Mon noon–4pm, Tue-Sat noon–2am, Sun noon–midnight; €€
Opposite the Philharmonie 2 in La Grande

Halle, this hip café-restaurant with an industrial-meets-greenhouse decor serves grilled meats and wood-oven pizzas and is a popular venue for concerts and other cultural events. Lovely terrace.

③ AU BŒUF COURONNÉ

188 avenue Jean-Jaurès, 19th; tel: 01 42 39 44 44; www.boeuf-couronne.com; daily; €€€
Outstanding restaurant, just across the road from where the meat market (now the music Conservatoire) used to be. Specialities include in every kind of steak, bone marrow with toast, and *tête de veau* (veal's head). Not for the faint-hearted.

Boating in the Bois de Vincennes

BERCY AND VINCENNES

Follow a pretty garden path along a former railway viaduct towards the regeneration quarter of Bercy. Choose between exploring the Bois de Vincennes or the old centre of the wine trade with its bars, cafés, cinemas and park.

DISTANCE: 7.25km (4.5 miles)
TIME: Half a day
START: Opéra Bastille
END: Parc de Vincennes or Bercy

Starting at the **Opéra National de Paris – Opéra Bastille ❶** (www.operadeparis.fr), walk down rue de Lyon and take avenue Daumesnil on your left. You will soon reach some steps, signposted Promenade Plantée. At the top begins a walk along a former railway viaduct now transformed into a garden.

Underneath the arches, dubbed the **Viaduc des Arts ❷** (1–129 avenue Daumesnil), are the shops of artisans and café **L'Arrosoir**, see ❶. At the end of the promenade is the **Jardin de Reuilly ❸**.

At this point, you have a choice: either continue along avenue Daumesnil

to the Bois de Vincennes, or head south to the Parc de Bercy and Bercy Village.

BOIS DE VINCENNES

If heading for the Bois de Vincennes, continue along avenue Daumesnil until you come to the **Palais de la Porte Dorée ❹** (www.palais-portedoree.fr; Tue–Fri 10am–5.30pm, Sat–Sun 10am–7pm) at no. 293, with its extraordinary basement aquarium

Inside the Musée des Arts Forains

and a cultural institute on the role of immigrants in France over the last 200 years.

Bois de Vincennes and Parc Floral

Continue on avenue Daumesnil to the **Bois de Vincennes** ❺ (daily 24/7; free), Paris's largest green space. Attractions include boating, cycle paths, a Buddhist temple, zoo (www.parczoologiquedeparis.fr; variable opening times, check online), hippodrome and theatre. The **Parc Floral** (charge) inside has a playground and crazy golf.

Château de Vincennes

On the northern edge of the park is the **Château de Vincennes** (www.chateau-de-vincennes.fr; 22 Sept–20 May: daily 10am–5pm, 21 May–21 Sept until 6pm), completed by Charles V in 1370 and now housing a museum.

BERCY

For the alternative option of **Bercy Village**, bear right after the Jardin de Reuilly onto rue de Charenton, and turn right onto rue Prudhon. Follow the road over the railway, past the church and onto the **Parc de Bercy** ❻ (May–Aug: Mon–Fri 8am–9.30pm, Sat–Sun 9am–9.30pm; late-Mar–Apr, Sept: Mon–Fri 8am–8.30pm, Sat–Sun 9am–8.30pm, Oct until 7.30pm, Nov–Feb until 6.30pm; free).

At the western end of the park is the rather ugly Ministère de l'Économie et du Budget and the AccorHotels Arena, a stadium and events venue. Also within the park is the Frank Gehry-designed **Cinémathèque Française** ❼ (51 rue de Bercy; www.cinematheque.fr; daily except Tue, see website for times): a film museum and film archive.

Bercy Village

As late as the 1980s wine was unloaded from barges at Bercy. Some *chais* (wine warehouses) have reopened as restaurants, wine bars and shops, others have been converted into the **Pavillons de Bercy** ❽, containing the **Musée des Arts Forains** ❾ (www.arts-forains.com; by appointment only), home to a collection of fairground music and Venetian carnival salons.

'NEW' LEFT BANK

Opposite Bercy on the so-called 'New' Left Bank is the **Bibliothèque Nationale de France – François Mitterrand** ❿. Its four 90m (295ft) -high glass towers are intended to evoke open books. The regenerated area is home to attractive bars and cafés, including several riverside ones.

Musée du Vin cellars

WESTERN PARIS

This is a posh part of town and off the main tourist track. Its attractions include pretty parks, Art Nouveau and Modernist architecture, Balzac's house and museums of wine and Impressionist art.

DISTANCE: 3.5km (2.25 miles)
TIME: A full day
START: Passy metro station
END: Musée Marmottan Monet or the Bois de Boulogne
POINTS TO NOTE: If you end the tour after the Musée Marmottan, pick up the metro at La Muette; if you continue to the Bois de Boulogne, the metro is at Porte Dauphine and Porte d'Auteuil.

The 16th *arrondissement* constitutes a sizeable slice of western Paris and is full of smart residences occupied by wealthy inhabitants. Just adjacent (though outside the Périphérique) is the Bois de Boulogne, an 860-ha (2,125-acre) expanse of woods and gardens laid out under town planner Baron Haussmann.

MUSÉE DU VIN

Catch the metro to Passy, and, as you leave the station, turn right down the steps. Turn right again at the bottom, then right a third time at rue des Eaux.

This street is named after the mineral springs where people came to take cures for anaemia in the days when Passy was a country village. Ironically, at the end of this street, at no. 5 square Charles-Dickens, is the **Musée du Vin ❶** (www.museeduvin paris.com; Tue–Sat 10am–6pm).

Here, within the cellars of a wine-producing monastery destroyed in the Revolution, you are guided through the wine-making process. There are also regular wine tastings (some in English) and a restaurant (Tue–Sat lunch only).

As you leave, turn right on to rue Charles-Dickens and walk straight on to the modest **Parc de Passy ❷**. Climb the steps on the north side of the park up to rue Raynouard and turn left.

MAISON DE BALZAC

On your left, at no. 47, is the newly reopened **Maison de Balzac ❸** (www.maisondebalzac.paris.fr; Tue–Sun 10am–6pm; permanent collection free). The writer Honoré de Balzac (1799–1850), a self-styled 'quill and ink galley slave', lived here in secret

Maison de Radio–France

for seven years, from 1840 (under the assumed name of Monsieur Breugnol, one of the characters in his novels) in order to escape his creditors. On the simple table in his study he worked day and night on *La Comédie Humaine*, his vast series of 91 novels and stories peopled with thousands of interconnected characters.

RADIO FRANCE

Now continue in the same direction on rue Raynouard to the **Maison de Radio-France ❹** (entrance on far side, at 116 avenue du Président-Kennedy; 1.5-hour tours, usually on Sat, by reserva-

tion only www.maisondelaradio.fr or tel: 01 56 40 15 16), the Orwellian home of the state radio station and broadcasting bureaucracy opened in 1963. Concerts, usually classical music, take place here every week.

ALTERNATIVE ROUTES

At this point you have a choice of routes. If you want to fast forward to the Musée Marmottan Monet (see page 87), turn right and walk up rue du Ranelagh. At the end of the road, go through the passage and turn right over the zebra crossing to the Jardins du Ranelagh. The museum is on the left, just off avenue Raphael.

Guimard's elaborate Castel Béranger

If, on the other hand, you are interested in taking a detour for an hour or so in order to see some fine examples of Art Nouveau and Modernist architecture, go up rue La Fontaine.

ARCHITECTURE TOUR

Art Nouveau
Rue Jean de La Fontaine is home to the city's best examples of Art Nouveau architecture by Hector Guimard, the man

---

Le Corbusier

Although Charles-Edouard Jeanneret (1887–1965), known as Le Corbusier, developed his brand of Modernism to provide better living conditions for inhabitants of crowded cities, he has been criticised for inspiring the building of soulless tower blocks surrounded by featureless wastelands. However, the two adjoining houses that make up the **Fondation Le Corbusier** (8/10 square du Dr Blanche; www.fondationlecorbusier.fr; Maison La Roche Mon 1.30–6pm, Tue–Fri 10am–12.30pm, 1.30–6pm, Sat 10am–6pm; guided tours in English at 4pm on Tue) show how elegant and light his buildings can be. Inside are exhibition spaces for his drawings, plans, furniture and paintings. It is also possible to visit his apartment in the nearby Immeuble Molitor (24 rue Nungesser et Coli, 16th; tel: 01 42 88 75 72; Mon, Tue, Fri 2–6pm, Sat 10am–1pm, 1.30–6pm).

---

who was responsible for the flamboyant entrances to metro stations such as the one at Abbesses (see page 66). On your right at no. 14 is the extraordinary **Castel Béranger ❺**, Guimard's first building commission, and he designed everything: the mosaic floors, the wallpaper, even the stoves. Despite its lavish decoration, Castel Béranger was built as a cheap lodging house.

Guimard also designed the more modest buildings at Nos 19 and 21, and the tiny **Le Berger & Les Poissons qui jouoïent de la flûte** (formerly Café Antoine) ❻ at No. 17 on your left. Further up, at No. 60, is the former **Hôtel Mezzara ❼**, currently closed and in the process of being bought with the aim of creating a homage to Hector Guimard's French Art Nouveau.

Soon after, turn right on to rue Ribera, which then becomes rue de l'Yvette.

Modernism
At the top of rue de l'Yvette is rue du Dr Blanche, with two examples of Modernist architecture. Turn left for square du Dr Blanche and the **Fondation Le Corbusier ❽** (see box) on your left. Next, turn right, and on your right is rue Mallet-Stevens, almost entirely made up of houses by Robert Mallet-Stevens (1886–1945). No. 10, with its stained-glass stairwell, is very fine.

Now continue north up rue du Dr Blanche and turn left at rue de l'Assomption, and then right on boulevard de Montmorency. Soon on your left is an inconspicuous path taking you through

Fondation Le Corbusier   *The Marmottan showcases Monet's work*

to avenue Ingres. Turn right and over the zebra crossing you will find the **Jardins du Ranelagh** ❾, an appealing park for young children, as it retains several old-fashioned carousels.

MUSÉE MARMOTTAN MONET

West of the gardens on the corner of rue Louis-Boilly (at no. 2) is the **Musée Marmottan Monet** ❿ (www.marmottan.fr; Tue–Sun 10am–6pm, Thur until 9pm), which gives an unrivalled overview of the career of Claude Monet (1840–1926). In the gallery downstairs, you start with *Impression, Soleil Levant (Impression, Sunrise)*, which gave the Impressionist Movement its name. Monet's ideas then evolve up to his last, almost abstract, *Nymphéas (Waterlily)* paintings.

Monet's contemporaries are also well represented. On the first floor are works by Pissarro, Renoir, Manet, Morisot, Caillebotte and Gauguin. On the ground floor, slightly incongruously, there is a fine collection of First Empire furniture and a section on medieval illuminated manuscripts.

PARKS AND GARDENS

With the route nearing its end, you have a choice of walking back through the Ranelagh gardens to cafés, restaurants and the metro home, or strolling through the vast **Bois de Boulogne** (24 hours; free) to the west beyond the Marmottan.

For the first option, walk back towards town along chaussée de la Muette. On the way you pass the **statue of La Fontaine** with the fox and crow from one of his fables and, as you leave the park, the lively **La Gare**, see ❶.

Bois de Boulogne

For the second option, if it is a pleasant summer evening, consider a meal at **Le Chalet des Îles**, see ❷. Otherwise, seek out **Les Serres d'Auteuil**, to the south (near the Roland-Garros tennis centre), all romantic glasshouses with orchids, begonias and palm trees, and the striking sails of the Frank Gehry-designed **Fondation Louis Vuitton** contemporary art centre (daily 10am–8pm) on avenue du Mahatma-Gandhi.

Food and drink

❶ LA GARE

19 chaussée de la Muette, 16th; tel: 01 42 15 15 31; www.lagare-paris.com; daily; €€€
Former railway station, where the ticket office has become the bar, and the platforms dining areas. Good-value lunch menus and there's brunch on Sundays.

❷ LE CHALET DES ÎLES

Lac Inférieur, Bois de Boulogne, 16th; tel: 01 42 88 04 69; www.chalet-des-iles.com; daily for lunch and dinner (Sun brunch only); €€€€
A short boat ride to the island on the more northerly of the park's two lakes leads to this pretty chalet, transplanted from Switzerland by Napoleon III. Gorgeous setting.

Tour Majunga (centre)

LA DÉFENSE

Named after a stand against the Prussians in 1870, La Défense is now a business district dominated by the Grande Arche, which completes the Royal Axis that links the Louvre, Tuileries, Champs-Élysées and Arc de Triomphe.

DISTANCE: 1.5km (1 mile)
TIME: 3 hours
START: Les Quatre Temps Shopping Centre, La Défense
END: Espace Culturel Raymond-Moretti
POINT TO NOTE: Take RER line A or metro line 1 to La Défense-Grande Arche.

La Défense was designated a business district as early as 1958, but it was not until the 1980s that its reputation was secured. Nowadays, more than 180,000 people work in the district, and about three-quarters of the top 20 French companies have their headquarters here, as do around a dozen of the top 50 companies in the world. And even though La Défense was officially completed in 1988 after 20 years' work, many of the original buildings are now being replaced with more advanced constructions.

Food and drink

❶ LE MOND
1 place des Corolles, 92400 Courbevoie; tel: 01 47 75 97 11; www.le-mond.fr
Mon–Fri; €€€
Classy restaurant with a shaded summer terrace where the (mainly business) clientèle enjoys seasonal market cuisine.

NEW DEVELOPMENTS

New buildings include the **Tour Majunga**, the **Tour D2** and the **Tour Carpe Diem**, all completed in 2013–14. The **Hermitage Plaza**, designed by Sir Norman Foster, will consist of two towers, one with 91 floors and the other with 89 floors, and will be the tallest building in the European Union at 323 metres (1,059ft) when it is completed in 2024. Other upcoming structures include the 167-metre (547ft) **Tour Trinity**, due in 2019 and the 150-metre (492ft) **Tour Alto**, due in 2020. And if other projects have been cancelled due to mount-

Lunch on the Arche's steps   *The Grande Arche*

ing costs, La Défense is nonetheless entering a new era.

GRANDE ARCHE

The metro exit brings you into **Les Quatre Temps ❶** shopping centre. Follow signs to the **Grande Arche ❷** (www.lagran dearche.fr; daily 10am–7pm). More than any other building, it is this great behemoth, designed by Danish architect Johan Otto von Spreckelsen, that put La Défense on the map, and in so doing became a symbol of François Mitterrand's 'progressive vision for the 1980s'.

Royal Axis and impressive statistics

From the steps of the arch, you can take in the Royal Axis that runs straight to the Arc de Triomphe, heads along the Champs-Élysées and Tuileries, and ends at the Arc de Triomphe du Carrousel and the Louvre. The size of the arch is symbolic, measuring 100m by 100m (330 sq ft), the same dimensions as the Cour Carrée at the Louvre.

SCULPTURE PARK

Wander down from the Grande Arche. On your left as you head southeast is the vaulted **CNIT ❸** (Centre National des Industries et des Techniques; 2 place de la Défense), a huge conference and exhibition centre.

Also here, seek out outdoor sculpture park **Le Musée à Ciel Ouvert ❹** (15 place de la Défense; always open; free), which includes works by Miró, César and Calder, as well as restaurant **Le Mond**, see ❶.

Walk down the esplanade du Général-de-Gaulle to reach the metro back into central Paris.

Rear view of the exquisite château

MALMAISON

In the quiet suburb of Rueil–Malmaison is one of the most appealing châteaux within easy reach of the French capital: Malmaison, the stylish and evocative former home of Josephine Bonaparte, first wife of Napoleon I.

DISTANCE: 24km (15 miles)
TIME: A full day
START: Château de Malmaison
END: Rueil-Malmaison
POINTS TO NOTE: The distance above is for the journey from Paris. By public transport take RER line A to La Défense-Grande Arche, then bus 258 to the 'Le Château' stop; by car, take RN 13 motorway from Paris.

To reach the **Château de Malmaison** ❶ (rue du Château; www.musees-nation aux-malmaison.fr; Oct–Mar 10am–12.30pm, 1.30pm–5.15pm, Sat–Sun until 5.45pm, park: 10am–6pm; Apr–Sep 10am–12.30pm, 1.30–5.45pm, Sat–Sun until 6.15pm, park: 10am–6.30pm), follow the instructions above.

BACKGROUND

The palace passed through various hands until, in 1799, it caught the eye of Madame Bonaparte. She engaged the services of up-and-coming architectural duo, Percier and Fontaine, to renovate the building in the fashionable neoclassical style, and in 1805 she employed L.M. Berthault to work on the park.

Country retreat and office

While Malmaison was initially used as a country retreat, by 1800 Napoleon was spending an increasing amount of her time here. But in 1809, since Josephine could not provide an heir, Napoleon nullified the marriage and gave his former wife the Malmaison estate. She stayed here until her death in 1814.

TOUR OF THE CHÂTEAU

Highlights on the **ground floor** include a monumental billiard table, two paintings by Gérard and Girodet, and Josephine's harp topped by an Imperial eagle. Also of note are Napoleon's striped, tent-style council room and the library with its classical-style busts of authors from Ovid to Voltaire.

Josephine and her children at Malmaison

First and second floors

The **first floor** houses the private apartments, although little of what is now on display is original and comes from other former royal residences. Most striking are the paintings of the couple by artists Gérard, Riesener, Bacler d'Albe and David. The **second floor** is dedicated to Josephine's impressive wardrobe.

THE GARDEN

Next, walk round to the back of the building to admire the park, beautifully landscaped in the English country-garden style. Still here is the massive cedar tree planted in 1800 to celebrate Napoleon's victory at Marengo.

OTHER ATTRACTIONS

A ticket for Malmaison also includes entry to The **Bois-Préau** Château (1 avenue de l'Impératrice Joséphine; Apr 9.30am–7pm, May–Sep 9.30am–8pm, Oct 9.30am–6pm, closed on Tue), the Napoleonic museum, and its park.

Also worth a pit stop are the **Pavillon Osiris** (Osiris Pavilion), with its decorative-arts collection, and the **Pavillon des Voitures** (Carriage Pavil-

ion), showcasing Napoleon's field landau used in his Russian campaign and the hearse used on St-Helena for his funeral.

It is a 15-minute walk into little **Rueil-Malmaison ❷**, where **Le Beauharnais**, see ❶, is an inviting option.

Food and drink

❶ LE BEAUHARNAIS

29 place de l'Église, Rueil Malmaison; tel: 01 47 51 02 88; Mon–Sun 6am–midnight; €
Nice brasserie in the church square with outdoor seating in summer.

Louis XIV, the Sun King

VERSAILLES

Described by the writer and philosopher Voltaire as 'a masterpiece of bad taste and magnificence', Versailles, symbol of pre–Revolutionary decadence, offers a vivid encounter with French history.

DISTANCE: 42km (26 miles)
TIME: A full day
START/END: Versailles
POINTS TO NOTE: To reach the palace by public transport take the RER line C to Versailles-Château–Rive Gauche station. By car: Versailles is 21km (13 miles) southwest of Paris by the A13 autoroute; take the exit No.5 Versailles Centre. Park on place d'Armes.

To reach the palace of **Versailles ❶** (www.chateauversailles.fr; Château: Apr–Oct Tue–Sun 9am–6.30pm, Nov–Mar Tue–Sun 9am–5.30pm. Petit Trianon, Hameau and Grand Trianon: Apr–Oct Tue–Sun noon–6.30pm, Nov–Mar Tue–Sun noon–5.30pm. Last entry 30 mins prior to closing. Gardens: Apr–Oct daily 8am–8.30pm, Nov–Mar daily 8am–6pm). Musical Fountains: Tue (mid-May–June), Sat and Sun (Apr–Oct). Musical Gardens: Tue (Apr–mid-May, July–Oct), Fri (Apr–Oct). Fountains Night Show: Sat (mid-June–mid-Sept) from central Paris, follow the instructions above.

BEGINNINGS

In 1623, Louis XIII, a passionate huntsman, built a lodge near the town of Versailles to the west of Paris, in order to take advantage of the thick forest in the area. In 1631, the king instructed his architect to upgrade the lodge.

Louis XIV
From 1661–8 further changes were made under the young Louis XIV by architect Louis Le Vau, painter Charles Lebrun and landscape gardener André Le Nôtre. Versailles was still too small, however, for king and entourage, so in 1668 Louis commissioned Le Vau to envelop the existing palace in a new building. From 1678, Jules Hardouin-Mansart took over as main architect, heralding a period of prolific building.

Official court residence
In 1682, Versailles became Louis XIV's official residence and the seat of the French government. New construction included the Hall of Mirrors, North and South wings, Stables, Grand Lodgings,

The Orangerie gardens *Lebrun oversaw this ceiling painting*

Orangery and Royal Chapel, as well as the redesign of the Grand Trianon.

Upon his proper accession to the throne after the Regency of 1715–22, Louis XV also kept court at Versailles. His architect, Ange-Jacques Gabriel, refurbished the private apartments and built the Petit Trianon (1762–4). Between 1768 and 1770 he also constructed the Royal Opera and in 1771 redesigned Mansart's crumbling North Wing in the classical French style.

REVOLUTION

The court under Louis XVI stayed at Versailles, keeping its distance from the increasingly discontented Parisian mob. This fantasy world was epitomised by the building of the Hameau (hamlet) for Marie-Antoinette between 1783 and 1787. Louis's world collapsed, however, when on 6 October 1789 he and his family were forced to return to the Palais des Tuileries in Paris. Louis, the last king in the Bourbon line, was guillotined on 21 January 1793.

NAPOLEON

After the Revolution, the palace was looted, and the estate fell into disrepair. Napoleon consid-

ered moving here, after his marriage in 1810 to his second wife, Archduchess Marie-Louise, but those plans never came to fruition. However, the couple did enjoy retreats in the Grand Trianon.

MUSEUM

Future occupants of the château did little to benefit it. Louis-Philippe of Orléans, who reigned 1830–48, carried out renovation work which took its toll on the buildings.

During the late 19th and the 20th century Versailles' main function was as a military headquarters: for the Germans during the Franco-Prussian War, for the Allied War Council during World War I, and then in World War II, from 1944 to 1945, for the Allies.

Palace ceiling

THE MAIN PALACE

Start the tour at the main palace, which can be visited without a guide. It includes the **Grands Appartements** (State Apartments) of the King and Queen, where the monarch's every move was scrutinised by a league of courtiers.

Here too is the **Galerie des Glaces** (Hall of Mirrors), ideally visited in the afternoon, when the sun streams in. Seventeen arched windows correspond to 17 mirrored arcades, and the vaulted ceiling features captions from the playwright Racine and 30 paintings by Lebrun of great events from the first 17 years of Louis XIV's 72-year reign. It was in this room that the Treaty of Versailles was signed to signify the official end of World War I.

A public way of life

The Versailles complex was designed to house the entire court and its entourage: some 20,000 people. Leaving their provincial châteaux or Parisian mansions, members of the nobility were obliged to spend years in service at court, at great personal expense, observing an elaborate system of etiquette in order to try to win the king's favour. Instead of plotting civil war, nobles fought for the honour of holding the king's shirt when he got out of bed in the morning during the celebrated public *levée*. Similarly, the king's meals were public ceremonies, and queens even gave birth in full view of courtiers.

For a supplement, you can see Louis XIV's private bedroom and the apartments of the Dauphin and Dauphine. Guided tours are offered for the private apartments of Louis XV, Louis XVI, Marie Antoinette, Madame de Pompadour and Madame du Barry, as well as the opera house and royal chapel.

TRIANONS AND HAMEAU

The two other main buildings on the estate are the Grand and Petit Trianons, located to the northwest, about 30 minutes on foot from the château. If you do not want to walk, take the mini train that runs regularly from the château, along the Grand Canal and across to the Trianons and back. Marie Antoinette's Hameau (classed, along with the Petit Trianon, as 'Marie Antoinette's Estate') is a cluster of thatched cottages, a 10-minute walk to the northeast.

Grand Trianon
The Italianate **Grand Trianon** ❷ was erected by Louis XIV as a miniature palace and haven from public life in the main château. Le Vau's original design of 1670 was replaced in 1687 with the marble architecture of Hardouin-Mansart that you see today. After being looted during the Revolution, the Grand Trianon was later redecorated in the Empire style for Napoleon and his second wife Marie-Louise. In more recent times, Charles de Gaulle stayed here during his presidency, and ever since, one wing has been reserved for the French Head of State.

The King's State Bedroom

Petit Trianon and Hameau

The **Petit Trianon** was built for Louis XV in the Greek style by Gabriel from 1762 to 1768 as a retreat for the king and his mistresses Madame de Pompadour, and later Madame du Barry. The gardens here were re-landscaped in the rambling English style for Marie Antoinette, who was given the Petit Trianon on her accession to the throne.

Also linked with Marie Antoinette is the **Hameau**, a cluster of thatched cottages by architect Richard Mique. The official Versailles guidebooks stress that these rustic-style buildings were not erected, as is popularly believed, so that the Queen could play at being a shepherdess, but as a dairy where food for the royal estate was produced.

THE GARDENS AND PARK

The château's 815ha (2,000 acres) of gardens and park are the work of André Le Nôtre, who created the ultimate French playground for Louis XIV out of unpromising hillocks and marshland.

A principal feature of the park is the **Grand Canal**, an ornamental stretch of water covering 44ha (105 acres), which can be explored by boat. Around the canal, a network of pathways, fountain basins, groves adorned with statuary, and sculpted trees and bushes, radiates out symmetrically. Look out for the **Orangerie**, with a vaulted gallery that could house over 2,000 orange trees, and the king's vegetable garden.

Fountain displays

Note that there is an extra charge for the gardens on Tuesdays, Saturdays and Sundays in season, when the fountains, powered by an ingenious hydraulic system, come to life and 17th-century music blasts over the *parterres*.

Eating

Of the cafés and restaurants within the grounds, two of the best are **La Flottille**, see ❶, and **La Petite Venise**, see ❷. There are also inexpensive open-air eating areas serving snacks in the groves on either side of the Latona Garden and Royal Avenue.

Food and Drink

❶ LA FLOTTILLE

Tel: 01 39 51 41 58; www.laflottille.fr; daily Apr–Oct 8am–8pm, Nov–Mar 8am–6pm; €€
At the head of the Grand Canal is this restaurant (serving standard French fare), brasserie and *salon de thé*.

❷ LA PETITE VENISE

Tel: 01 39 53 25 69; www.lapetitevenise.com; daily 11.45am–6pm (low season until 5.30pm and closed Mon); €€€
Located between the Bassin d'Apollon and the Grand Canal, this Italian restaurant has contemporary décor and wines from Sicily, Tuscany and Venice. Under Louis XIV, this was the workshop where the royal gondolas were built.

The stunning entrance to the château

FONTAINEBLEAU

Louis IX called Fontainebleau his 'wilderness', François I referred to trips here as 'coming home', and, from exile in St Helena, Napoleon Bonaparte called it 'the true home of kings'. Little wonder that, like Versailles, it is a World Heritage Site.

DISTANCE: 120km (74miles)
TIME: A full day
START/END: Fontainebleau
POINTS TO NOTE: The distance above is from Paris. To reach the palace by train: from the Gare de Lyon to Fontainebleau-Avon (45mins), then 'Château' bus from the station or 30min walk through town. By car: take the Fontainebleau exit on the A6 autoroute; the château is 16km (10 miles) away. Parking is available in the town.

Close to the town centre of Fontainebleau is the **Château de Fontainebleau** ❶ (place Général-de-Gaulle; www.chateaudefontainebleau.fr; Wed–Mon Oct–Mar 9.30am–5pm, Apr–Sept until 6pm; courtyard and gardens Nov–Feb 9am–5pm, Mar–Apr, Oct until 6pm and May–Sept until 7pm; park 24/7), the only fully furnished royal palace in France.

BACKGROUND

In 1528, to indulge his passion for blood sports, François I commissioned a pal-ace in the Mannerist style on the site of a medieval royal hunting lodge near the 100-sq km (40-sq mile) Forêt de Fontainebleau. Just back from his conquests in Italy, François introduced France to the Renaissance style, which became known as the First Fontainebleau School.

Palace evolution

Renovations and additions were carried out under Henri II, Henri IV, Louis XIV and Louis XVI, but with the latter came the French Revolution, and the palace was no longer the home of kings. It was stripped of its contents and left to ruin, until 1803, when Napoleon founded a military school here and began a full refurbishment.

Food and drink

❶ LE BACCHUS
4 rue Richelieu, Hôtel Le Richelieu, Fontainebleau; tel: 01 64 22 26 46; €€
Tasty and varied cuisine using fresh local ingredients. Outdoor terrace is a bonus.

The Louis XVI wing

During the Bourbon Restoration (1815–30), Louis-Philippe continued the renovation, followed, in the Second Republic, by Napoleon III. In the late 19th century Empress Eugénie added new salons and a Chinese Museum. From 1945 to 1965 NATO had its military headquarters here.

PALACE TOUR

The entrance is on the right-hand side of the **Cour du Cheval Blanc** (White Horse Courtyard), as you face the double-horse-shoe staircase. This is the Louis XV wing, which houses the **Musée Napoléon I**, showcasing clothing, weapons, accessories and paintings relating to the emperor.

First floor

At the end of this wing, ascend the stairs to the **Grands Appartements** (State Apartments) and Renaissance rooms. Highlights include the Galerie François I, emblazoned with his initials and heraldic salamander, the ballroom and the Salon Louis XIII. Also superb is the Galerie de Diane and the king's bedroom, turned in 1808 into a throne room, as well as Napoleon's elegant Imperial Apartment.

Ground floor

The tour continues on the ground floor, with the 16th-century **Chapelle de la Trinité**, in which Louis XV was married in 1725. Ahead are the modest **Petits Appartements**, Napoleon's private suite.

You can also visit Empress Eugénie's salons and the **Musée Chinois** (Chinese Museum; closed 11.30am–2.30pm).

The garden

Highlights in the grounds include the early 19th-century English garden, the carp pond, the Grand Parterre, the canal and what is still the largest *jeu de paume* (real-tennis court) in the world.

BACK TO TOWN

After your visit, exit via the main gate, cross place d'Armes and then head along rue du Château (which eventually becomes rue Grande). **Le Bacchus**, see ❶, is a good spot to eat in town.

Monet's house

GIVERNY

A visit to Monet's house, at Giverny in Normandy, is an exercise in retinal pleasure. Gardens brimming with flowers, a Japanese bridge, waterlilies and a pink house: it's easy to see why he proclaimed it 'a splendid spot for me'.

DISTANCE: 160km (100 miles)
TIME: A full day
START: Fondation Monet
END: Musée des Impressionnismes
POINTS TO NOTE: To reach the start point by train: from the Gare St-Lazare to Vernon (45 mins) trains are infrequent, so check times in advance (www.sncf.com); at Vernon take a shuttle bus 15 mins to the village (leaves the station about 15 mins after the arrival of Paris train); or, rent a bike from opposite the station (around €15 per day, 25 mins ride on the flat; see www.fondation-monet.com for details of the route). By car: take the A13 west to Bonnières, then the D201 to Giverny.

Claude Monet (1840–1926) discovered Giverny, where the Seine meets the river Epte, in 1883, spying it from the door of the little train that used to run at the bottom of what is now the Clos Normand garden. He moved here with his own two children, his mistress Alice Hoschedé (his wife had died of tuberculosis in 1879) and her six children, and lived here for 43 years until his death.

In the early years, Monet was desperately short of money, and his art dealer, Durand-Ruel, helped him pay the rent. Eventually, though, the painter prospered: he purchased this house, married Alice, and laid out the gardens you see today at great expense.

FONDATION MONET

From the car and coach parks, it is just a hop to 84 rue Claude-Monet and the **Fondation Monet** ❶ (www.fondation-monet.com; Mar 23–Nov 1 daily 9.30am–6pm). Beyond the ticket booth, you reach the museum shop, once one of the many studios that Monet built around the property, and used for the production of the waterlily paintings, *Les Nymphéas*, now in the Musée de l'Orangerie (see page 36) in Paris.

The house
After the shop, on the right, is Monet's eccentrically coloured house: pink and green on the outside, while inside the din-

His 'Japanese Bridge'

Waterlilies in the Water Garden

ing room is bright yellow, and the kitchen is sky blue. Upstairs, the bedrooms are light and airy, with big windows on to the gardens. The walls of the rooms feature Japanese prints from his extensive collection.

Food and drink

❶ LA BRASSERIE DES ARTISTES

99 rue Claude-Monet; tel: 02 32 21 52 21; www.brasseriedesartistes.fr; Mon–Sun 10am–5.30pm; €€

This restaurant offers typical French menu (like onion soup, crêpes or moules) inspired by regional specialities. You can eat here without a museum ticket.

❷ HÔTEL BAUDY

81 rue Claude-Monet; tel: 02 32 21 10 03; Mar–Nov daily 10am–9.30pm; €€

Once the focal point for the village's American artists, this hotel has a restaurant that does classic French food.

The garden

The garden is already familiar to many from Monet's paintings. Immediately in front of the house is the grid pattern of flowerbeds of the Clos Normand. Below is the Water Garden, for which Monet bought the land in 1893. Obtaining official permission to dig his ponds was a protracted business, but by 1895 Monet was able to have his waterlilies, the Japanese bridge, the willows and the pond with punt. In 1966, Monet's son Michel bequeathed the property to the state.

MUSÉE DES IMPRESSIONNISMES

After your visit of the gardens, turn left out of the Fondation and walk along rue Claude-Monet. At no. 99 is the **Musée des Impressionnismes** ❷ (www.mdig. fr; end-Mar–mid-Nov daily 10am–6pm; closed two weeks in July), devoted to American artists, who, inspired by the Movement, came to Giverny. You can lunch here at **La Brasserie des Artistes**, see ❶, or further along at **Hôtel Baudy**, see ❷.

Monet was initially receptive to the arrivals, but tired of the invasion: 'When I first came to Giverny I was quite alone, the little village was unspoiled. Now, so many artists, students, flock here, I have often thought of moving away.' As you leave, you may feel some sympathy.

Sleeping Beauty's Castle

DISNEYLAND PARIS

If your children are tired of art museums, and unimpressed with another lunch of foie gras, then Disneyland Resort Paris may be in order. Here, they can enjoy all the latest fairground rides and as many burgers as they can eat.

DISTANCE: 64km (40 miles)
TIME: At least a full day
START/END: Disneyland
POINTS TO NOTE: The distance above is from central Paris. Directions on how to get to the park are as follows: by public transport, catch the RER A from central Paris at Auber, Châtelet or Étoile to Disneyland Resort Paris (Marne-la-Vallée/Chessy station); by car, take the A4 east of Paris to Marne-la-Vallée (exit 14), where there are signs to the resort and car parks.

Located on a 83-ha (205-acre) site at Marne-la-Vallée, east of Paris, **Disneyland Resort Paris** ❶ (daily, but opening times vary considerably: for bookings and information, see www.disneylandparis.com) covers an area one-fifth of the size of Paris. On average, it welcomes around 14 million visitors annually – more than any other amusement park in Europe. While, visitors come from all around the world most are from France (around 48 percent) and Britain (around 15 percent). Given the amount to see, families might

consider spreading a visit over two days. The on-site hotels are costly, but staying on the spot means early access to the attractions. The park's official language is English, but French is widely spoken.

Homecoming

According to the Disney marketing machine, Disneyland Paris was something of a homecoming; Walt's family came from Isigny-sur-Mer in Normandy, and the name d'Isigny (from Isigny) became Disney in the US. But financial governmental incentives, not family history, were behind the final decision to bring Disney to Europe.

The complex has three parts: the main park, Walt Disney Studios (a self-contained park that offers a behind-the-scenes look at the history of animation, film and television) and the hotels and shops of Disney Village.

THE MAIN PARK

Disneyland's 'imagineers' have created five 'magic lands': **Fantasyland**, the most popular area for children, with boat trips,

Disney Village   *Inside the Nautilus, of Jules Verne fame, in Discoveryland*

carousels and a hedge maze; **Main Street USA**, representing the early 1900s, with ragtime and Dixieland bands (though also featuring Sleeping Beauty's Castle); **Frontierland**, evoking the wild west; **Adventureland**, with characters such as Captain Hook; and the futuristic **Discoveryland**, which has Star Wars Hyperspace Mountain, and French-themed attractions, such as an underwater trip that pays homage to celebrated French sci-fi writer Jules Verne's *20,000 Leagues Under the Sea*.

WALT DISNEY STUDIOS

Disneyland Resort Paris celebrated its 10th anniversary in 2002 by opening up **Walt Disney Studios ②**, which has four studio lots to entice visitors. Directly through the entrance is Front Lot, a mock

film set of a street. There's also Production Courtyard, giving an insight into the production process; this is the site of the Studio Tram Tour, a ride that lets you see what it feels like to be slap-bang in the middle of the filming action.

Then there's Backlot, which documents stunts and special effects – a great area for older children, teens, and adults. And lastly there's Toon Studio, which goes back to basics with pen and paper to explain how animated classics are made.

DISNEY VILLAGE

The wider resort, **Disney Village**, is a celebration of 'Americana' and home to the resort hotels. Hotel Cheyenne is the most imaginative: a film-set Western hotel, with saloon, sheriff's jail and wooden-planked stores. Several hotels overlook Lake Disney, including Hotel New York, offering luxury rooms in a Manhattan-style skyscraper.

The jewel in the park's crown is the elegant Victorian-style Disneyland Hotel, while in a forest 5km (3 miles) from the main park is Davy Crockett Ranch, where accommodation comprises camping and caravanning places and log cabins, with bike hire available.

DIRECTORY

Hand-picked hotels and restaurants to suit all budgets and tastes, organised by area, plus select nightlife listings, an alphabetical listing of practical information, a language guide and an overview of the best books and films to give you a flavour of the city.

ACCOMMODATION

Paris has more rooms than almost any other city in Europe with hotels ranging from the pint-sized to the palatial. Most hotels in the centre are concentrated in the 8th *arrondissement* (around the Champs-Élysées), the 9th (around the Opéra and Grand Magasins) and in the 10th (near the Gare du Nord). There are few hotels in the budget range – most are in the two- and three-star category. Don't expect to find a bargain – in general, it's hard to find anything really good, with its own bathroom, for less than 100 euros. In the middle range, the stress is generally on style and charm rather than high-tech facilities.

An alternative to staying in a hotel is a bed and breakfast. Several companies organise home stays. Alcôve & Agapes Bed & Breakfast à Paris (www. bed-and-breakfast-in-paris.com) has more than 100 homes on its register. Bed and Breakfasts Paris (www.bed breakfast-paris.com) has a collection of some of the best rooms throughout the city.

> Price for a double room for one night without breakfast:
> €€€€= over 300 euros
> €€€ = 200–300 euros
> €€ = 100–200 euros
> € = below 100 euros

Hotel prices in Paris are not subject to restrictions and can be changed without notice, so check before booking. The majority of hotels vary prices by season. State your arrival time if you book by phone, or your room may not be held after 7pm.

Not all properties are wheelchair-accessible; even if a hotel does have an elevator, for example, it is likely that it will be a fairly small one. Travellers with disabilities should check before reserving. All hotels have Wi-fi, unless stated.

The Islands

Hôtel des Deux-Îles
59 rue St-Louis-en-l'Île, 4th; tel: 01 43 26 13 35; www.deuxiles-paris-hotel.com; metro: Pont Marie; €€€€
A peaceful and attractive hotel in a 17th-century mansion house in the Île St-Louis. Some rooms have views over a pretty courtyard.

Hôtel du Jeu de Paume
54 rue St-Louis-en-l'Île, 4th; tel: 01 43 26 14 18; www.jeudepaumehotel.com; metro: Pont Marie; €€€–€€€€
Delightfully set on the pretty Île St-Louis, this hotel, with ancient beams, has had a contemporary makeover but still retains its charm. Breakfast is served in the mansion's 17th-century real-tennis court (hence

Elegant hotel sign

the name). Bar, library, concierge, room service until 10pm and an attractive courtyard garden.

Hôtel Lutèce

65 rue St-Louis-en-l'Île, 4th; tel: 01 43 26 23 52; www.paris-hotel-lutece.com; metro: Pont Marie; €€€

The Lutèce has the same owners as the Hôtel des Deux-Îles, and is similarly charming, rich in 17th-century beams and stonework. The wood-panelled sitting room has a superb fireplace, and rooms are decorated in warm colours.

Louvre, Tuileries and Concorde

Hôtel Brighton

218 rue de Rivoli, 1st; tel: 01 47 03 61 61; www.paris-hotel-brighton.com; metro: Tuileries; €€

This hotel has several rooms that overlook the Jardin des Tuileries, and a reception area awash with gilt, marble and glass chandeliers. Rooms are large and decorated with a mix of traditional quality fabrics, careful lighting and sober furniture and artworks. The rooms with the fine views are understandably popular, so book well ahead.

Hôtel Costes

239 rue St-Honoré, 1st; tel: 01 42 44 50 00; www.hotelcostes.com; metro: Tuileries; €€€€

This hip hotel is just off elegant place Vendôme in an exclusive neighbourhood lined with chic boutiques. The rooms are exquisitely decorated with Baroque paintings, heavy drapes and antiques. Some bathrooms have claw-foot bathtubs and mosaic tiles. The hallways are lit with candles; even the indoor pool, which has an underwater sound system, is dark. Other facilities include a bar, restaurant, swimming pool and spa, perfume shop, room service and parking.

Grand Hôtel du Palais Royal

4 rue de Valois, 1st; tel: 01 42 96 15 35 www.grandhoteldupalaisroyal.com; metro: Palais Royal; €€€€

In an 18th-century building in the southeastern corner of the elegant Palais Royal is this intimate luxury hotel, which opened its doors in 2013. The 68 rooms and suites, some with their own balcony, successfully marry classical style with contemporary lines; the Terrace Suite unsurprisingly has its own terrace with great views over the city. As well as a restaurant and bar, there's also a spa, which uses Carita products and has a Turkish bath, and a fitness centre.

Opéra and Grands Boulevards

Banke Hotel

20 rue La Fayette, 9th; tel: 01 55 33 22 22; www.hotelbanke.com; metro: Chaussée d'Antin – La Fayette, Gare St-Lazare; €€€

Located in the heart of the Grands Boulevards, in the imposing Hauss-

The five-star Plaza Athénée

mannian former headquarters of the Crédit Commercial de France (CCF) bank, this hotel screams luxury and comfort, right from the vast domed reception area. There are 91 sound-proofed rooms, which are richly decorated in chocolates, purples, reds and creams, reminiscent of a gentleman's club, with highlights of gold; those on the 6th floor have views of the Sacré-Cœur and the Palais-Garnier. Facilities include several restaurants (including the Josefin, which offers Spanish dishes), a bar, gym and spa. There's even a private art collection.

Hôtel Chopin

10 boulevard Montmartre (46 passage Jouffroy), 9th; tel: 01 47 70 58 10; www.hotelchopin-paris-opera.com; metro: Grands Boulevards; €

Tucked away at the end of an historic 19th-century glass-and-steel-roofed arcade, this is a quiet, friendly and simply furnished hotel, offering 36 rooms at a fabulous price for the location. Facilities are basic, but there are televisions in the rooms, and they are en suite. Book well in advance.

Hôtel Langlois

63 rue St-Lazare, 9th; tel: 01 48 74 78 24; www.hotel-langlois.com; metro: Trinité; €€

If you fancy stepping back in time then this three-star hotel is the place for you. Rooms are decorated in Belle Époque and Art Nouveau style, each furnished with individual antiques and paintings, each with original features dating from 1870 when the building was constructed. The continental breakfast isn't cheap (around 15€) but it's worth trying just to check out the old-fashioned birdcage in the breakfast room. You can also choose to have breakfast served in your own room.

Hôtel Mansart

5 rue des Capucines, 1st; tel: 01 42 61 50 28; www.paris-hotel-mansart.com; metro: Madeleine, Opéra; €€

Named in honour of Jules Hardouin-Mansart, architect to Louis XIV, this is good value for the location, just off über-chic place Vendôme. The lobby is decorated with abstract murals inspired by French formal garden designs, and the spacious, high-ceilinged rooms are furnished with antiques and oil paintings; the duplex Vendôme suite looks out over the square itself.

Hôtel Plaza Athénée

25 avenue Montaigne, 8th; tel: 01 53 67 66 65; www.dorchestercollection.com; metro: Alma Marceau; €€€€

This palatial hotel, with lavish mostly Louis XVI- or Regency-style decor, has sound-proofed rooms, a club, gym, 'Dior Institut' spa and an eponymous restaurant headed by super-chef Alain Ducasse. If you can't stretch to the price of a room, treat yourself to a cocktail in the fashionable bar.

A modern option

The charming Caron de Beaumarchais

W Paris – Opéra

4 rue Meyerbeer, 9th; tel: 01 77 48 94 94; www.wparisopera.com; metro: Chaussée d'Antin-La Fayette; €€€€

In a grand 1870s building near the Opéra, this establishment does not compromise comfort for style: it is famous for its beds (the two Extreme Wow Suites have circular ones) and Egyptian cotton linen. All rooms have big-screen TVs, rainforest showers and iPod docking stations. Chill out at Bar Brûlé or try some gourmet food in Coquette restaurant.

Marais

Hôtel de la Bretonnerie

22 rue St-Croix-de-la-Bretonnerie, 4th; tel: 01 48 87 77 63; www. hotelparismaraisbretonnerie.com; metro: St-Paul, Hôtel de Ville; €€

Historic features abound in this delightful Marais hotel set in a 17th-century *hôtel particulier*. The rooms and suites are all furnished with lavish fabrics and rich colours; some have wooden beams and romantic four-poster beds.

Hôtel Caron de Beaumarchais

12 rue du Vieille du Temple, 4th; tel: 01 42 72 34 12; www.carondebeaumarchais. com; metro: St-Paul, Hôtel de Ville; €€

A gorgeous little hotel in an excellent location in one of the nicest streets in the Marais. Rooms are decorated in the romantic French 18th-cen-

tury style with pretty chandeliers and antiques, in honour of the 18th-century playwright after whom the hotel is named. Friendly management. There are only 19 rooms, so book in advance.

Hôtel Duo

11 rue du Temple, 4th; tel: 01 42 72 72 22; www.duo-paris.com; metro: Hôtel de Ville; €€€

Trendy hotel in a great spot in the Marais, just steps from the Hôtel de Ville. The 58 rooms, which are quiet despite the central location, thanks to excellent sound-proofing, are furnished in contemporary style, with good-sized bathrooms (unusual in Paris). Facilities include a bar, gym and sauna.

Hôtel Jules & Jim

11 rue des Gravilliers, 3rd; tel: 01 44 54 13 13; www.hoteljulesetjim.com; metro: Arts et Métiers, Temple; €€€

This super-cool, LGBTQ-friendly hotel pays homage to François Truffaut's famous film of the same name. The 23 stylish-yet-simple rooms (think wood, glass and stone) are based in three buildings around two courtyards.

Pavillon de la Reine

28 place des Vosges, 3rd; tel: 01 40 29 19 19; www.pavillon-de-la-reine.com; metro: St Paul, Chemin Vert; €€€€

View from the top of Terrass in Montmartre

This romantic mid-sized hotel, located on the elegant place des Vosges, feels like a chic country château. Rooms vary greatly in size and price, but most have four-poster beds, exposed wooden beams and antiques. There's also a cosy lobby bar with evening wine tasting, and manicured gardens, plus the Spa de la Reine, with fitness room, Jacuzzi, treatment booths and steam room.

Hôtel du Petit Moulin

29 rue du Poitou, 3rd; tel: 01 42 74 10 10; www.hotelpetitmoulinparis.com; metro: St-Sébastien Froissart, Filles du Calvaire; €€

This fashionable hotel in the Marais was designed by Christian Lacroix using sumptuous fabrics and screen-printed *trompe l'œil* to create comfort and individuality. The reception occupies an old bakery, still with its painted glass ceiling panels, while the bar marries zinc counter, murals and pop colours.

Hôtel de la Place des Vosges

12 rue de Birague, 4th; tel: 01 42 72 60 46; www.hotelplacedesvosges.com; metro: St Paul; €–€€

An intimate hotel with only 16 rooms in a former stables. It's popular and in a great location by the place des Vosges, so book ahead. A successful marriage of old and new, although still slightly crumbly. Friendly staff.

Champs-Élysées, Trocadéro and West

Hôtel Daniel

8 rue Frédéric Bastiat, 8th; tel: 01 42 56 17 00; www.hoteldanielparis.com; metro: St-Philippe du-Roule, Franklin D. Roosevelt; €€€€

A member of the prestigious Relais & Châteaux group, the upmarket Hôtel Daniel is wonderfully romantic, with rooms exquisitely decorated with chinoiserie wallpaper, plush carpets and pretty antiques. Facilities include a bar, restaurant, parking and room service. An excellent location for the Champs-Élysées and rue du Faubourg St-Honoré.

Four Seasons George V

31 avenue George V, 8th; tel: 01 49 52 70 00; www.fourseasons.com/paris; metro: George V, Alma Marceau; €€€€

One of the most famous hotels in Paris, just off the Champs-Élysées. The George V offers the height of opulence, with beautifully decorated, traditional-style rooms with modern touches and magnificent marble bathrooms. Facilities include a fabulous spa inspired by the palace at Versailles, a bar, three restaurants, including three Michelin-starred Le Cinq, and a business centre. Exquisite service.

La Maison

8 rue Jean-Goujon, 8th; tel: 01 40 74 64 64; www.lamaisonchampselysees.com;

Budget-friendly Hôtel Chopin

metro: Champs-Élysées-Clémenceau, Franklin Roosvelt; €€€€
Ultra-stylish 40-room hotel in a Haussmannian building with minimalist interiors by fashion designer Martin Margiela. Enjoy a cocktail in The Blind Bar, light up in The Cigar Bar or savour a copious brunch on Sundays. There is a restaurant with a nice outside terrace too.

Plaza Tour Eiffel Hotel

32 rue Greuze, 16th; tel: 01 47 27 10 00; www.plazatoureiffel.com; metro: Trocadero; €€–€€€
This four-star boutique hotel is located between the Eiffel Tower and the Champs-Élysées and offers 41 comfortable, well-furnished rooms. Friendly team, 24/7 room service and a fitness room.

Hôtel de Sers

41 avenue Pierre 1er de Serbie, 8th; tel: 01 53 23 75 75; www.hoteldesers-paris. fr; metro: Alma Marceau; €€€€
The Sers combines modern style and comfort with the classic service of a traditional small French hotel. It has brushed-concrete floors downstairs, an interior courtyard with perpetually changing coloured light washes, modern furniture and very sleek bathrooms. But young architect Thomas Vidalenc has cleverly warmed up the minimalism with lots of lilac and crimson in carpets and curtains, as well as a witty nod to its Belle Époque origins in the gallery of portraits in the hallway.

Hôtel de la Trémoille

14 rue de la Trémoille, 8th; tel: 01 56 52 14 00; www.tremoille.com; metro: Alma Marceau; €€€€
This discreetly elegant hotel has been thoroughly modernised yet retains its sense of Parisian style – 19th-century panelling, mouldings and fireplaces meet contemporary lighting and fabrics, and the comforts of air conditioning, internet access and so on. There's a fitness room and spa facilities in the basement. It's a calm hideaway, and you can even have your breakfast dispatched to you in privacy through a hatch in the door. Attached is the similarly elegant Le Louis^2 bar and restaurant.

Montmartre

Hôtel Amour

8 rue de Navarin, 9th; tel: 01 48 78 31 80; www.hotelamourparis.fr; metro: St-Georges; €€–€€€
Trendy boutique hotel in the style of an exclusive English gentleman's club, with 24 rooms decorated by contemporary artists; some of them even feature art installations. The bar has DJs, and the pretty restaurant has a garden.

Hôtel Particulier

23 avenue Junot, 18th; tel: 01 53 41 81 40; www.hotel-particulier-montmartre.

com; metro: Lamarck-Caulaincourt, Abbesses; €€€€

Gorgeous small hotel in a townhouse on one of the most desirable streets in Paris. The five suites are individually decorated with antiques, design classics and sumptuous fabrics. Dinner, by reservation only, is available Tue–Sat. A great place to get away from it all.

Hôtel Royal Fromentin

11 rue Fromentin, 9th; tel: 01 48 74 85 93; www.hotelroyalfromentin.com; metro: Blanche, Pigalle; €€

A hotel not far from Pigalle with its own special touches typical of the neighbourhood: the lobby was formerly a cabaret dating from the 1930s, "The Don Juan", and it still has the original wood panelling and some appropriate cabaret paraphernalia. Several of its 47 rooms have views of the Sacré-Cœur; the decor is bright but fairly traditional, and rooms are spacious and clean. There's a vintage glass lift, too.

Terrass

12–14 rue Joseph-Maistre, 18th; tel: 01 46 06 72 85; www.terrass-hotel.com; metro: Abbesses; €€€

From the hotel rooftop restaurant (and some of the rooms) you can enjoy one of the most spectacular views of Paris. This has been "the address of artists since 1911" and staying here allows you can follow in Dali's, Matisse's and Edith Piaf's footsteps. Enjoy one of the 92 recently completely renovated and redesigned to recall an artist's dressing room.

Hôtel Beaumarchais

3 rue Oberkampf, 11th; tel: 01 53 36 86 86; www.hotelbeaumarchais.com; metro: Filles du Calvaire; €

A fun, good-value designer hotel located in the trendy Oberkampf district, with plenty of nightlife nearby. The rooms are painted in bright, primary colours. There's a terrace for breakfast in summer, and public car park nearby; 31 rooms.

Best Western Saint Martin Bastille

114 boulevard Richard-Lenoir, 11th; tel: 01 43 38 29 29; www. hotelsaintmartinbastille.com; metro: Oberkampf; €€

This affordable hotel is a perfect base for the dedicated bar-hopper, as it's on the corner of rue Oberkampf, still one of the liveliest nightlife hubs in the city. Five of the 27 rooms are singles; some rooms are classical, some quite unusual, but all have air conditioning and Wi-fi; breakfast is served in a vaulted basement.

Hôtel Garden St Martin

35 rue Yves-Toudic, 10th; tel: 01 42 40 17 72; www.hotelgardenrepublique.com; metro: Jacques Bonsergent; €€

Situated near the Canal St-Martin, a little off the beaten track, this is a val-

Eastern Paris offers more budget options than elsewhere in Paris

ue-for-money hotel with a small garden terrace and an even smaller lift. All the rooms are clean and compact.

Le Général

5–7 rue Rampon, 11th; tel: 01 47 00 41 57; www.legeneralhotel.com; metro: République; €€€

This hotel offers the boutique experience at reasonable(ish) prices. The rooms are beautifully decorated, minimalist yet cosy. There's a gym, a sauna and a bar. Room service is available 24/7.

Mama Shelter

109 rue de Bagnolet, 20th; tel: 01 43 48 48 48; www.mamashelter.com; metro: Gambetta, Porte de Bagnolet; €–€€€

Located slightly off the beaten track, just east of Père Lachaise cemetery, this Philippe Starck-designed hotel is billed as a 'sensual refuge'. It's large (170 rooms) and industrial in style, but the biggest surprise is the price, with rooms from around 90 euros. Rooms are stylish and contemporary with their own entertainment systems. Facilities include a restaurant, a pizzeria, two chic bars and a shop selling such indispensable items as toothbrushes and phone chargers.

Hôtel Original

8 boulevard Beaumarchais, 11th; tel: 01 47 00 91 50; www.hoteloriginalparis.com; metro: Bastille; €€€

The latest offering from fashion designer Stella Cadente is in a great location between places des Vosges and place de la Bastille. The 37 rooms in this ultra-modern boutique hotel have been individually and colourfully decorated and possess all mod cons including an iHome docking station and plasma TV.

Le Pavillon Bastille

65 rue de Lyon, 12th; tel: 01 43 43 65 65; www.pavillonbastille.com; metro: Bastille; €€

Classy, contemporary hotel situated behind an attractive courtyard opposite the Opéra Bastille. Decor is modern and well kept, and facilities and services are excellent. Popular with business people.

The Latin Quarter and St-Germain

Abbaye St-Germain

10 rue Cassette, 6th; tel: 01 45 44 38 11; www.hotelabbayeparis.com; metro: St-Sulpice; €€€–€€€€

This 17th-century abbey is excellently situated between the Jardin du Luxembourg and St-Germain-des-Prés, and has been sensitively converted into a hotel. The old-style decor, such as the beams and wood panelling, is charming, but there are all modern conveniences, too. Breakfast is served in the garden in summer by attentive staff. Facilities include room service and a bar.

Hôtel d'Angleterre

44 rue Jacob, 6th; tel: 01 42 60 34 72; www.hotel-dangleterre.com; metro: St-Germain, Rue du Bac; €€€

This delightful hotel was the site on which the Treaty of Paris, proclaiming the independence of the US, was prepared in 1783; during the 19th century it was used as the British Embassy. Ernest Hemingway lodged here (in room 14) in 1921. The rooms are fairly small and furnished with antiques; only the top-floor doubles are spacious. There's a lovely terrace and garden, where breakfast is served in summer.

Le Clos Médicis

56 rue Monsieur-le-Prince, 6th; tel: 01 43 29 10 80; www.closmedicis.com; metro: Cluny-Sorbonne, RER Luxembourg; €€

This stylish boutique hotel in an 18th-century *hôtel particulier* near the Jardin du Luxembourg offers chic bedrooms, antique tiles in the bathrooms, fabulous flower arrangements, an open fire in the lounge in winter and helpful staff. There's also a courtyard garden.

Hôtel Esmeralda

4 rue St-Julien-le-Pauvre, 5th; tel: 01 43 54 19 20; www.hotel-esmeralda.fr; metro: St-Michel, Maubert Mutualité; €

The 17th-century Esmeralda, the ultimate in shabby chic, is one of those places you either love or loathe. Its 16 rooms have loud floral wallpaper (probably peeling off the walls), antique furniture (some say 'flea-ridden') and a rickety old staircase (no elevator) that takes some negotiating with suitcases. In addition to their low prices (rooms from around 80 euros for a single) and the undeniable character, the attraction is the incredible location; just under half of the rooms have views of Notre-Dame directly across the Seine.

Meliá Paris Notre-Dame

7 rue de l'Hôtel Colbert, 5th; tel: 01 56 81 19 00; www.melia.com; metro: Cluny-La Sorbonne, Maubert-Mutualité; €€€

A romantic hotel set in a 16th-century building at the foot of Notre-Dame. The rooms are chic and there is a good breakfast buffet and charming garden.

Hôtel de Nesle

7 rue de Nesle, 6th; tel: 01 43 54 62 41; www.hoteldenesleparis.com; metro: Odéon, Pont Neuf; €

A laid-back student and backpackers' hotel. Facilities are basic, but the 18 rooms (nine are en suite) are cheerfully decorated with murals, furnished according to eclectic themes and spotless. There is a garden with a pond, and a hammam.

Hôtel Le Six

14 rue Stanislas, 6th; tel: 01 42 22 00 75; www.hotel-le-six.com; metro: Vavin or Notre-Dame-des-Champs; €€€

Design-conscious but child-friendly boutique hotel where the rooms

The Pavillon de la Reine, on place des Vosges

have iPod/iPhone docks, Nespresso machines and L'Occitane toiletries. Relax after a hard day's sightseeing with a drink in the glass-roofed lounge, book a massage or a beauty treatment in the Le Six & Spa or ease away aches and pains in the hammam. No restaurant but there is room service.

The 7th

Le Saint

3 rue du Pré-aux-Clercs, 7th; tel: 01 42 61 01 51; www.lesainthotelparis.com; metro: St-Germain-des-Prés; €€€

This trendy hotel in the up-market 7th arrondissement has 54 uniquely decorated spacious rooms and suites. Amenities include a bar, a restaurant, a wellness centre and room service. There is also a private chauffeur service and a gift shop.

Hôtel de Verneuil

8 rue de Verneuil, 7th; tel: 01 42 60 82 14; en.hotel-verneuil-saint-germain.com; metro: St-Germain, Rue du Bac; €€–€€€

A cosy, characterful hotel in an elegant 17th-century building in the up-market 7th arrondissement, with small but attractive rooms. Singer Serge Gainsbourg lived just opposite, and the wall outside his old house is decorated with graffiti in homage. Well placed for St-Germain. The hotel also has a smart apartment nearby.

Le Walt

37 avenue de La Motte-Picquet, 7th; tel: 01 45 51 55 83; www.lewaltparis.com; metro: Ecole Militaire; €€€€

This boutique hotel certainly has the glam factor: 25 rooms decorated in classic or contemporary style – some of which have views of the Eiffel Tower, and all of which have sleek glass-and-chrome bathrooms and large oil paintings over the bed – combine with wooden floors and a stylish little courtyard restaurant.

Montparnasse

Hôtel Louison

105 rue de Vaugirard, 6th; tel: 01 53 63 25 50; www.louison-hotel.com; metro: Montparnasse-Bienvenüe; €€€

A little winter garden and a characterful lounge and reception area set the tone at this carefully put-together establishment. The 42 elegant rooms and one stand-alone apartment have recently been completely renovated and are spread over six floors and two buildings. Book online to get the best deals.

La Maison Montparnasse

53 rue de Gergovie, 14th; tel: 01 45 42 11 39; www.lamaisonmontparnasse.com; metro: Pernety; €€

The owners of this lovely hotel are keen that guests should feel at home, hence the name. Take your pick from 36 contemporary rooms where pink, yellow, purple or orange are the dominant colour schemes. Breakfast can be taken on the terrace in summer.

Classic brasserie Le Grand Colbert

RESTAURANTS

France's dedication to the gastronomic arts is legendary, and the respect for food in all its forms is still strongly in evidence in the capital. Granted, it may not be as cheap as it once was to dine out here – even the classic set menus can seem pricey these days – but that doesn't seem to have deterred either Parisians or tourists. The city is peppered with great eateries, from bistros, brasseries and glitzy Michelin-starred restaurants to Breton crêperies and Moroccan couscousseries and top-notch Asian restaurants, all of which affords plenty of opportunity to sample life as a true *bon viveur*. Note that in up-market restaurants there is often a dress code, with a jacket requested and tie preferred for men. Note, too, that many restaurants close on Sunday evening (brasseries are the useful exception to this) and for the whole of August.

The Islands

Le Sergent Recruteur

41 rue St-Louis-en-l'Île, 4th; tel: 01 43 54 75 42; www.lesergentrecruteur.fr; closed Mon and Sun; metro: Pont Marie; €€€€

Price guide for dinner for one with half a bottle of house wine:
€€€€ = over 60 euros
€€€ = 40–60 euros
€€ = 25–40 euros
€ = under 25 euros

Stylish and fashionable restaurant in ancient surroundings where chef Antonin Bonnet puts a contemporary twist on French market cuisine.

Louvre, Tuileries and Concorde

Le Grand Véfour

17 rue de Beaujolais, 1st; tel: 01 42 96 56 27; www.grand-vefour.com; closed Sat–Sun and Aug; metro: Palais-Royal; €€€€
Hiding under the arches of the Palais-Royal is one of the most beautiful restaurants in Paris. Le Grand Véfour opened its doors in 1784 and has fed the likes of Emperor Napoleon and writers Alphonse Lamartine, Colette, and Victor Hugo. Today it serves haute cuisine under the aegis of chef Guy Martin, Classics include foie gras raviolis with a truffle sauce.

Opéra and Grands Boulevards

Aux Lyonnais

32 rue St-Marc, 2nd; tel: 01 42 96 65 04; www.auxlyonnais.com; closed Sat lunch, Sun, Mon and Aug; metro: Grands Boulevards; €€€
Founded in 1892, this bistro still retains its original decor but has been beautifully revamped under top chef Alain Ducasse. The menu pays tribute to Lyonnaise specialities, with renditions of pike, perch and crayfish quenelles. Other highlights include frogs' legs, charcuterie, excellent cuts of beef and regional wines.

Leave space for dessert · *Expect haute cuisine at Le Grand Véfour*

Chartier

7 rue du Faubourg Montmartre, 9th; tel: 01 47 70 86 29; www.bouillon-chartier.com; daily 11.30am–midnight; metro: Grands Boulevards; €

Chartier is the best-known low-price eatery in town. The atmosphere is an experience in itself, with Belle Époque decor, snappy waiters, shared tables and plenty of bonhomie. Arrive early if you want to stand a chance of getting a seat as there are no bookings.

Gallopin

40 rue Notre-Dame-des-Victoires, 2nd; tel: 01 42 36 45 38; www.gallopin.com; daily noon–2.30pm and 7pm–10.30pm; metro: Bourse; €€€

This brasserie opposite the Stock Exchange opened in 1876 and is still decorated in Belle Époque style. The chef prepares refined versions of traditional dishes, including *pâté maison*, *steak tartare* and flambéed crêpes. The fish is a star attraction, with specialities such as haddock poached in milk with spinach, and delicious seafood platters. Excellent food in a distinguished setting.

Le Grand Colbert

2 rue Vivienne, 2nd; tel: 01 42 86 87 88; www.legrandcolbert.fr; daily noon–12.30am, (until 10.30pm in August); metro: Bourse; €€€

This large, beautiful brasserie, which opened in 1830, offers the sort of traditional dishes that the French have always demanded from their brasseries. Choose from beef carpaccio, goat's cheese in pastry, sole meunière, Burgundian snails or frogs' legs in garlic, ripe cheeses, and creamy chocolate mousse and feathery light *îles flottantes* (soft meringues floating in custard).

Taillevent

15 rue Lamennais, 8th; tel: 01 44 95 15 01; www.letaillevent.com; closed Sat, Sun and Aug; metro: George V; €€€€

One of the most illustrious haute-cuisine restaurants in Paris, with one Michelin star, but still surprisingly unstuffy. The food is magnificent: the earthy signature, spelt, is cooked 'like risotto' with bone marrow, black truffle, whipped cream and parmesan and is truly heavenly. Jacket requested.

The 7th

L'Ami Jean

27 rue Malar, 7th; tel: 01 47 05 86 89; www.lamijean.fr; Tue–Sat; metro: Tour Maubourg, Invalides; €€€€

This recently redesigned restaurant offers distinct and innovative cuisine. The chef, Stéphane Jégo, is ever present to talk and joke with his customers. If you do not want to wait in line for a table you can order a takeaway online.

L'Arpège

84 rue de Varenne, 7th; tel: 01 47 05 09 06; www.alain-passard.com; Mon–Fri; metro: Varenne; €€€€

Chef Alain Passard has been called 'the poet of *terroir*' for his imaginative menus and signature dessert of tomato *confite* with 12 seasonings (should you be able

Super-chef Alain Ducasse is at the helm of Aux Lyonnais

to name all of them you may even get the dish for free). Three Michelin stars.

L'Atelier de Joël Robuchon

5 rue de Montalembert, 7th; tel: 01 42 22 56 56; www.joel-robuchon.com; lunch and dinner daily; metro: Rue du Bac, St-Germain-des-Prés; €€€€

Even jaded Parisians queue up in all weathers to sample the warm *foie gras* brochettes or tapenade with fresh tuna conjured up by one of France's most revered chefs. The restaurant is built around an open kitchen, so you can watch the masters at work, and the atmosphere is slick, like that of a bar. Reservations are advised. Two Michelin stars.

Au bon Accueil

14 rue de Monttessuy, 7th; tel: 01 47 05 46 11; www.aubonaccueilparis.com; Mon–Fri; metro: Ecole Militaire; €€€

The decor here is sophisticated and elegant, with a lightness of touch; likewise the cooking. The *prix-fixe* dinner menu (around €37) is exceptional value. Sit on the terrace for views of the Eiffel Tower.

Le Florimond

19 avenue de la Motte-Picquet, 7th; tel: 01 45 55 40 38; www.leflorimond.com; Mon–Fri; metro: Ecole Militaire, Latour Maubourg; €€–€€€

Pascal Guillaumin's bistro has a cosy, intimate atmosphere. His traditional French dishes are beautifully presented, and the service is warm and friendly. There's a great-value three-course set menu

at lunch time for around €27.50; the evening set menu is €40.

Champs-Élysées and Trocadéro

Alain Ducasse au Plaza Athénée

25 avenue Montaigne, 8th; tel: 01 53 67 65 00; www.ducasse-paris.com; lunch Thu–Fri, dinner Mon–Fri, typically closes around Christmas and New Year and for a month during the summer; metro: Alma-Marceau; €€€€

Cooking elevated to an art form from globetrotting chef Alain Ducasse, France's first recipient of six Michelin stars (three apiece for two restaurants), with the help of his acolyte Christophe Moret. According to Ducasse, his meals are not about fancy presentation but purity and essence of flavour. Expect truffles in abundance but also superb vegetables from Provence, where he first made his name. Jackets essential for men; tie recommended.

Le Cinq

31 avenue George V, 8th; tel: 01 49 52 71 54; www.restaurant-lecinq.com; daily lunch and dinner; metro: George V; €€€€

The Four Seasons Hotel George V restaurant offers a transcending though very expensive food experience from chef Christian Le Squer – thoroughly deserving its three Michelin stars. Attentive service and superb wine list.

L'Entredgeu

83 rue Laugier, 7th; tel: 01 40 54 97 24; www. lentredgeu.fr; lunch and dinner Mon–Fri, Sat

Simple but elegant soup

lunch only; metro: Porte de Champerret; €€

The unpronounceable name and non-central location apart, this superior bistro has a lot going for it. Dishes include roast duckling in honey sauce and lots of foie gras, and the decor is suitably cosy and intimate.

Minipalais

3 avenue Winston Churchill, 8th; tel: 01 42 56 42 42; www.minipalais.com; daily 10am–2am; metro: Champs-Élysées-Clemenceau; €€€

In the majestic surroundings of the Grand Palais, in a high-ceilinged room decorated with contemporary furniture, are served traditional dishes with a modern twist created by acclaimed chef Eric Frechon: try the duck *foie gras* burger drizzled with truffle *jus* followed by a simple strawberry and apple salad. The terrace, under a magnificent colonnade, is a delight on sunny days. A good place for just a drink too.

Le Pré Catelan

Le Pré Catelan, Bois de Boulogne, 16th; tel: 01 44 14 41 14; www.leprecatelan.com; closed Sun and Mon, typically two weeks in March, three weeks in Aug and last week in Oct; metro: Porte Maillot; €€€€

In the heart of the Bois de Boulogne, this is one of the most romantic spots in Paris. Frédéric Anton prepares spectacular haute cuisine centring on fresh truffles, lobster, lamb and fresh seafood. Reserve in advance.

Le Roi du Pot-au-feu

34 rue Vignon, 9th; tel: 01 47 42 37 10;
closed Sun and typically mid-July–mid-Aug; metro: Madeleine; €

Traditional bistro (think red-and-white checked tablecloths) specialising in *pot-au-feu*. Once a rural stew eaten by peasant farmers, it is now a fashionable dish among Parisian gourmets. The best part is the bone marrow. Other French classics are also well executed here.

La Table Lauriston

129 rue Lauriston, 16th; tel: 09 74 56 22 23; www.latablelauriston.com; closed Sat lunch, Sun and Aug; metro: Trocadéro; €€€

A bright, modern, award-winning bistro with traditional French cuisine such as terrine of pigs' trotters, frogs' legs in parsley sauce and lemon tart. The lunch menu is good value (around €30 for three courses) and there is an extensive wine list, with the emphasis on smaller producers.

Beaubourg and Les Halles

Au Pied de Cochon

6 rue Coquillière, 1st; tel: 01 40 13 77 00; www.pieddecochon.com; open 24/7; metro: Louvre-Rivoli, Châtelet; €€€

In its heyday, this 24/7 brasserie catered for market workers; now it is rather more upmarket. Still, the house speciality remains the same: grilled pig's trotter with Béarnaise sauce. Other star turns include the oysters and the onion soup (good for hangovers).

Benoît

20 rue St-Martin, 4th; tel: 01 42 72 25 76; www.benoit-paris.com; lunch and dinner daily,

Talking through the specials

closed Aug; metro: Hôtel de Ville, Châtelet; €€€€

At this vintage bistro, renowned for its excellent cooking and high prices, master chef Alain Ducasse offers timeless terrines and casseroles. A very chic affair.

La Fresque

100 rue Rambuteau, 1st; tel: 01 42 33 17 56; www.lafresqueparis.com; closed Sun; metro: Les Halles; €–€€

Sitting elbow to elbow at one of the big wooden tables is part of the charm here, as is the decor (white faïence tiles, frescoes, etc). The bistro fare, such as beef stew and duck, is excellent, and the staff are friendly. Always one vegetarian main course.

Le Petit Marcel

65 rue Rambuteau, 4th; tel: 01 48 87 10 20; daily; metro: Rambuteau; €€

Inside, the walls are lined with Art Nouveau tiles and the ceiling is painted; outside, there is seating on the terrace. The menu comprises standard French fare – salads, steak frites, omelettes, tarts – but all well prepared, inexpensive and tasty.

Marais and Bastille

404

69 rue des Gravilliers, 3rd; tel: 01 42 74 57 81; www.404-resto.com; lunch and dinner daily, Sat–Sun brunch; metro: Arts et Métiers; €€

Packed, hip and atmospheric, with low seating and iron grilles on the windows casting lacy patterns through the dim interior on to the tables. The Moroccan menu features filo-pastry pies, lamb brochettes, an exotic selection of couscous and tagines, and fragrant Berber desserts. The bar, Andy Wahloo, is a popular watering hole.

Auberge Pyrénées-Cévennes

106 rue de la Folie-Méricourt, 11th; tel: 01 43 57 33 78; www.auberge-pyrenees-cevennes. fr; closed Sun and Sat lunch, and typically most of Aug and first week in Jan; metro: République; €€€

There's a reason why this classy spot won a best bistro award: the waiters are friendly, the decor is unique (purple-and-white cloths, terracotta floors, and stuffed animal heads on the wall), and the hearty food is top-notch. Try lentil caviar or *frisée aux lardons* (salad with bacon), followed by cassoulet, pigs' feet, fish quenelles, and baba au rhum or profiteroles.

Breizh Café

109 rue Vieille-du-Temple, 3rd; tel: 01 42 72 13 77; www.breizhcafe.com; Mon–Sun 10am–11pm; metro: Filles du Calvaire; €

Owned and run by a Breton, this popular crêperie offers a good selection of *galettes* (savoury buckwheat pancakes) and crêpes (sweet pancakes) made with organic flour. Try one with *andouille* (chitterling sausage) accompanied by a Breton cola or *lait ribot* (buttermilk). Vegetarians won't go hungry.

Le Dôme du Marais

53bis rue des Francs-Bourgeois, 4th; tel: 01

Bistrot Paul Bert   *Gourmet Le Comptoir*

42 74 54 17; www.ledomedumarais.fr; closed Mon–Tue; metro: Rambuteau; €€€

Unstuffy restaurant in a grand setting (once the auction house for the state-owned pawnbrokers). Beautifully executed seasonal market cuisine and a great place for Sunday brunch.

Robert et Louise

64 rue Vieille du Temple, 4th; tel: 01 42 78 55 89; www.robertetlouise.com; Mon–Thur dinner, Fri–Sat lunch and dinner; metro: Saint-Paul; €€

This cosy restaurant with its roaring fire is a carnivore's delight: superb black pudding, steak served on a wooden platter and thick, tasty beef stew.

Le Souk

1 rue Keller, 11th; tel: 01 49 29 05 08; closed Mon; metro: Ledru-Rollin; €€€

Excellent atmospheric Moroccan restaurant that serves up hearty, spiced cuisine. Choose from huge tagines, plentiful couscous plates and succulent lamb shanks followed by delicate pastries and end with a palate-cleansing mint tea. Plenty of vegetarian options and good-value lunch menus.

Latin Quarter/St-Germain

Le Comptoir

9 carrefour de l'Odéon, 6th; tel: 01 44 27 07 97; daily; metro: Odéon; €€€

This gourmet bistro is one of the most desirable addresses in the area so book in advance. Next door, the more affordable Avant Comptoir offers wine by the glass as well as platters of charcuterie and other nibbles.

La Cuisine de Philippe

25 rue Servandoni, 6th; tel: 01 43 29 76 37; closed Sun and Mon; metro: St-Sulpice; €€€

Opposite the Jardin du Luxembourg, this charming little bistro serves traditional French dishes. Savoury and sweet soufflés are the house speciality.

La Fourmi Ailée

8 rue du Fouarre, 5th; tel: 01 43 29 40 99; www.parisresto.com; daily; metro: Maubert-Mutualité; €

Ambient, inexpensive, haven of a tea-room-cum-restaurant that was formerly a women's library (the walls are still lined with books).

Le Timbre

3 rue Sainte-Beuve, 6th; tel: 01 45 49 10 40; www.restaurantletimbre.com; closed Sun, Mon and typically in Aug, Wed only lunch; metro: Vavin, Notre-Dame-des-Champs; €€–€€€

Located near the Jardin du Luxembourg, in a vibrant, foodie-friendly area of the 6th dubbed the 'Quartier Vavin', British-born Christopher Wright's postage stamp-sized ('timbre' means stamp) eatery uses market-fresh produce to serve up French classics with an English twist. The well-executed set menu of three courses, costing around €40 per person and including service but not wine, has won rave reviews from critics in France and back across the Channel.

Montmartre

L'Annexe

13 rue des Trois Frères, 18th; tel: 01 46 06
12 48; www.lannexe-paris18.fr; closed Wed,
Mon–Tue, Thur dinner only, Fri–Sun lunch and
dinner; metro: Abbesses; €€€

Cosy place run by two young women, one
is the chef and the other is the sommelier,
offering traditional French dishes including *tartare* (raw minced beef). Vegetarian
and vegan options are available.

Chez Toinette

20 rue Germain-Pilon, 18th; tel: 01 42 54 44
36; Mon–Sat from 7pm; metro: Abbesses;
€€€

Where many places in this part of town
fob off unwitting tourists with overpriced
fare, this amiable bistro has a good, well-
priced blackboard menu that runs to
steaks, wild-boar terrine, a lovely warm
goat's cheese salad and prunes soaked
in Armagnac.

The East and Northeast

Bistrot Paul Bert

18 rue Paul Bert, 11th; tel: 01 43 72 24 01;
closed Sun, Mon and Aug; metro: Faidherbe-
Chaligny; €€€

This bustling bistro is one of the best
places in Paris to enjoy steak and chips.
The menu is traditionally French, with a
wide range of desserts including home-
made raspberry *macarons* and the house
speciality, a *Paris-Brest*. The wine menu
is extensive, catering for all tastes and
budgets, and a large number of wines are
available by the glass.

Le Pavillon du Lac

Parc des Buttes Chaumont, 19th; tel: 01 42
00 07 21; www.lepavillondulac.fr; Tue–Sat
10am–11.pm, Sun until 7.30pm; metro:
Buttes-Chaumont; €€€

Café-restaurant in a lovely setting next to
the park's lake. Good-value set menus
and Sunday brunch

Le Train Bleu

1st floor, Gare de Lyon, 12th, tel: 01 43 43 09
06; www.le-train-bleu.com; lunch and dinner
daily; metro: Gare de Lyon; €€€€

In the midst of the Gare de Lyon, the ter-
minus for trains from the Mediterranean,
this huge, impressive brasserie was built
for the 1900 World Fair. With its frescoed
ceilings depicting destinations served by
the trains from the station, mosaics and
gilt detailing, it is Second Empire style at
its very grandest. Classic French dishes
are well prepared and efficiently served.
Good-value set menus.

Le Verre Volé

67 rue de Lancry, 10th; tel: 01 48 03 17 34;
www.leverrevole.fr; daily 12.30–2.30pm
and 7.30–10pm; metro: Jacques Bonsergent;
€€

This wine shop-cum-restaurant close to
the Canal St-Martin is cosy inside, with
cheery green wooden chairs and dinky
tables packed together. Wine bottles line
the walls – you can choose from a small
number by the glass or else just pay a
corkage charge on any of the 300 or so
bottles for sale. The food is classic French
fare.

La Coupole, a Montparnasse institution

Zoé Bouillon

66 rue Rébéval, 19th; tel: 01 42 02 02 83; Mon, Tue, Sat lunch only, Wed–Fri lunch and dinner, Sun dinner only; metro: Pyrénées; €

Healthy soups and salads are the specialities here. Great for vegetarians.

Western Paris

Chez Géraud

31 rue Vital, 16th; tel: 01 45 20 33 00; www.lacauserie.fr Mon–Fri lunch and dinner; metro: La Muette; €€€

Classic bistro serving hearty regional cuisine, with the emphasis on roasted meat and game dishes. Excellent service.

Zebra Square

3 place Clément Ader, 16th; tel: 01 44 14 91 91; www.zebra.paris daily 7.30–midnight; metro: Ranelagh; €€€

In Hotel Square, this stylish restaurant has a traditional menu with a nod towards the Mediterranean. Try the custardy *tarte tropézienne* for dessert.

Montparnasse and the 'New' Left Bank

Chai 33

33 cour St-Emilion, 12th; tel: 01 53 44 01 01; www.chai33.com; daily; metro: Cour St-Emilion; €€

Innovative restaurant in a former wine warehouse. Choose your wine from six styles, from light with a bite to rich and silky, with well-executed fusion food to match. Unpretentious sommeliers are on hand to help.

Côté Sushi

378 rue de Vaugirard, 15th; tel: 01 84 17 25 26; www.cotesushi.com; daily 11am–3pm and 6–11pm; €€

This restaurant specialises in Nikkei cuisine – a subtle blend of Peruvian cuisine, spicy and colourful, with Japanese technique and flavours. Chirashi and poke bowls also feature on the extensive menu. Fresh food, a friendly team, and good value.

La Coupole

102 boulevard du Montparnasse, 14th; tel: 01 43 20 14 20; www.lacoupole-paris.com; Mon 8am–11.30pm, Tue–Fri 8am–midnight, Sat 8.30am–midnight, Sun until 11.30pm; metro: Vavin; €€€

This legendary Art Deco brasserie (the largest in Paris) opened its doors in 1927 and is still going strong. Now run by the Flo Brasserie group, it has a convivial atmosphere, and its popularity remains intact. The classic brasserie fare includes huge platters of shellfish, *choucroute* and Alsatian sausages, and steaks and hearty stews.

La Régalade

49 avenue Jean-Moulin, 14th; tel: 01 45 45 68 58; closed Sat, Sun, Mon lunch; metro: Alésia; €€€

A destination bistro for epicures across Paris for over 10 years, La Régalade never disappoints. Since taking over the reins, chef Bruno Doucet has injected it with life, while retaining much of what was good about it, especially the reasonable pricing. *Prix-fixe* menu is €37.

NIGHTLIFE

Paris is legendary as a city of culture, with theatres, concert halls, cinemas, cabaret halls and clubs to suit every taste, housed in anything from an Art Deco palace to former Turkish baths.

Theatre

Comédie Française

1 place Colette, 1st; tel: 08 25 10 16 80 (from France)/ +33 1 44 58 15 15 (from outside France); www.comedie-francaise.fr; metro: Palais-Royal

Since 1799, France's national theatre has performed at this fine neoclassical building by the Palais Royal. Most productions are in the classical repertoire, by playwrights such as Corneille, Molière and Racine, although plays by more modern classic writers are also shown.

Odéon – Théâtre National de l'Europe

Place de l'Odéon, 5th; tel: 01 44 85 40 40; www.theatre-odeon.fr; metro: Odéon

This grand neoclassical behemoth stages classics, translations of foreign works, and contemporary drama – anything from Alexandre Dumas to new commissions.

Dance

Ballet de l'Opéra National de Paris

Bastille: 120 rue de Lyon, 12th; Palais-Garnier: Place de l'Opéra, 9th; tel: 08 92 89 90 90 (from within France)/+33 1 71 25 24 23 (from elsewhere); www.operadeparis.fr; metro: Bastille (for the Opéra Bastille) or Opéra (for the Palais-Garnier)

Classics and new productions are staged by the Ballet de l'Opéra under current dance director Aurélie Dupont. Most are shown in the sumptuous 19th-century Palais Garnier (see page 46), although some are performed at the more modern Opéra Bastille (see page 57).

Théâtre National de Chaillot

Palais de Chaillot, 1 place du Trocadéro, 16th; tel: 01 53 65 31 00; www.theatre-chaillot.fr; metro: Trocadéro

This Art Deco complex houses three auditoria, mostly used for global dance performances, although also some drama.

Music

Caveau de la Huchette

5 rue de la Huchette, 5th; tel: 01 43 26 65 05; www.caveaudelahuchette.fr; metro: St-Michel

Established in 1946, this jazz and swing club was frequented by GIs during World War II and has been going strong ever since, with big names such as Claude Bolling and Sacha Distel having performed here.

Opéra National de Paris, Bastille and Palais-Garnier

For details, see pages 57 and 46

The Opéra Bastille is the Opéra National's main venue for operatic productions, with acclaimed conductor Philippe Jordan the current Musi-

A Lido show

cal Director. Fans under 28 can enjoy cheap prices if they turn up on the day and there are still seats available.

Philharmonie de Paris

221 avenue Jean-Jaurès, 19th; tel: 01 44 84 44 84; www.philharmoniedeparis.fr; metro: Porte de Pantin

The Jean Nouvel-designed Philharmonie de Paris is the city's new music hub holding concerts, exhibitions, conferences and more, with a symphonic hall seating 2,400. The adjacent Philharmonie 2 (formerly the Cité de la Musique) has two auditoriums and a Museum of Music.

Film

Le Balzac

1 rue Balzac, 8th; tel: 01 45 61 02 53; www. cinemabalzac.com; metro: George V

This stylish retro cinema shows the latest films as well as older films by season (silent movies, etc). Also hosts concerts.

Cinémathèque Française

51 rue de Bercy, 12th; tel: 01 71 19 33 33; www.cinematheque.fr; metro: Bercy

The headquarters of French cinema are based in a building designed by Frank Gehry. The Cinémathèque has a repertory cinema, a bookshop, restaurant, museum, research centre and archive.

Cabarets

Le Lido

116 avenue des Champs-Élysées, 8th; tel: 01 40 76 56 10; www.lido.fr; metro: George V, Franklin D. Roosevelt

The famous 'Bluebell Girls' high-kick their way through the Lido's spectacular shows with countless costume changes, 23 sets and a myriad of special effects. Probably the grandest of the cabaret shows.

Moulin Rouge

82 boulevard de Clichy, 18th; tel: 01 53 09 82 82; www.moulinrouge.fr; metro: Blanche

Marvel at the 'Doriss' dancers as they parade to perfection in magnificent costumes dripping with feathers, sequins and rhinestones. Prices are steep but it's crazily over the top and fun.

Clubs

Le Divan du Monde

75 rue des Martyrs, 18th; tel: 01 40 05 08 10; www.divandumonde.com; metro: Abbesses, Pigalle

This 19th-century former music hall, once frequented by Baudelaire and Toulouse Lautrec, is now a hip club and live-music venue featuring an eclectic range of music. There is usually some cabaret before it turns into a late-night dance club.

Bus Palladium

6 rue Pierre Fontaine, 18th; tel: 01 45 26 80 35; www.lebuspalladium.com; metro: Pigalle

Once frequented by Dalí, Gainsbourg and The Beatles and now hip again.

Le Rex Club

5 boulevard Poissonnière, 2nd; tel: 01 42 36 10 96; www.rexclub.com; metro: Bonne Nouvelle

A techno, house and drum 'n' bass stalwart, aimed at hard-core clubbers.

A great way to get around

A–Z

A

Addresses

Paris is divided into 20 numbered districts, called *arrondissements* because they fan out in a 'round' pattern, clockwise from the city centre. Officially they are labelled by a five-digit postcode (75001, 75002, etc), but most people refer to them by their abbreviated form (1st, 2nd, 3rd, 4th, etc).

B

Bicycles

Some 20,000 bikes, in around 1,100 racks, across Paris can be used by anyone through the city's Vélib' Metropole (from 'vélo libre' or 'bike for free') scheme: www.velib-metropole.fr. For frequent users the company offers a subscription plan. Short-term visitors can buy a 1 or 7 day pass (see page 132), and pedal away (the first half an hour is free).

Business hours

Traditionally, **banks** open from Monday to Friday 9/9.30am to 5/5.30pm and are closed on weekends. However, many now open on Saturday.

Most **boutiques** and **department stores** open between 9 and 10am, closing at around 8pm or later (for the big shopping malls). **Food shops**, especially bakers, open earlier. Lunchtime closing is increasingly rare; most shops do, however, close on Sunday, but bakers and patisseries usually open in the morning.

C

Climate

The average maximum in July and August is 25°C (77°F), the average minimum 15°C (59°F), but 27°C (81°F) is not unusual. In January, expect a maximum of 6°C (43°F), a minimum of 1°C (34°F).

Clothing

Paris is a great city to explore on foot, so comfortable walking shoes are essential. Bring warm clothes if you're visiting in winter, as the weather can be very chilly, and remember to have something waterproof (or at least an umbrella) with you in spring or autumn, as showers are quite common.

Size conversions

Women: 38 (UK 8/ US 6), 40 (UK 10/US 8), 42 (UK 12/US 10), etc. Men: suits: subtract 10, so a French 46 is equivalent to a UK or US 36. Shirts: 36 (14 UK/US), 37 (14.5), 38 (15), etc.

Crime and safety

In the event of loss or theft, a report must be made in person at the nearest police station *(commissariat)* as soon as possible. See www.prefecturedepolice.inter

Boulangeries open early in the morning

ieur.gouv.fr for addresses of stations; for emergency help tel: 17 or 112.

If you lose your passport, report it to your consulate straight after notifying the police. There is a list of consulates (consulats) in the local *Yellow Pages (Pages Jaunes)*, see www.pagesjaunes.fr.

Security: It is advisable to take the same precautions in Paris as you would in any other capital city, notably watching out for pickpockets on public transport and shielding your PIN at ATM machines. Known centres of prostitution (such as parts of the Bois de Boulogne) are best avoided at night. It is advisable to take extra caution in the areas around metro Les Halles, Châtelet, Gare du Nord, Stalingrad, Jaurès, and the northern Paris suburbs late at night.

Expect extra security checks at airports and major attractions. Be aware that suitcases, travel bags and backpacks exceeding 55 x 35 x 20cm (21 x 14 x 8ins) will not be allowed in most museums and cannot be left at cloakrooms.

Customs regulations

Visitors of all nationalities must declare, upon arrival or departure, sums of cash exceeding €10,000 (or equivalent).

Duty-Paid Goods: If you are an EU resident and buy goods in France on which you pay tax, there are no restrictions on the amounts you may take home with you. However, EU law has set 'guidance levels' on the amounts that are acceptable of the following, and if you exceed these amounts you must be able to show that the goods are for personal use:

Spirits: 10 litres
Fortified wine/wine: 90 litres (not more than 60 litres may be sparkling)
Beer: 110 litres.

Duty-Free Goods: If you are from outside the EU and buy goods duty-free in France, the following limits still apply (these quantities may be doubled if you live outside Europe):

Tobacco: 800 cigarettes, or 400 cigarillos, or 200 cigars, or 1kg of tobacco
Alcohol: 1 litre of spirits/liqueurs over 22 percent volume, or 2 litres under 22 percent. 4 litres still wine and 16 litres beer
Perfume: 50g of perfume, plus 250ml of eau de toilette. Up to a value of €430 for air and sea travellers; up to value of €300 for other travellers.

E

Electricity

You will need an adaptor for most British and US plugs: French sockets have two round holes. Supplies are 230 volt, and US equipment will need a transformer.

Embassies/Consulates

Australia: 4 rue Jean-Rey, 15th; tel: 01 40 59 33 00; www.france.embassy.gov.au.
Canada: 130, rue du Faubourg Saint-Honoré, 8th; tel: 01 44 43 29 00; www.canadainternational.gc.ca.
New Zealand: 103 rue de Grenelle, 7th; tel: 01 45 01 43 43; www.mfat.govt.nz.
Republic of Ireland: *Embassy*: 12 avenue Foch, 16th; tel: 01 44 17 67 00; www.dfa.ie.

The two main French newspapers

South Africa: 59 quai d'Orsay, 7th; tel: 01 53 59 23 23; www.afriquesud.net.

UK: *Consulate*: 18bis rue d'Anjou, 8th; tel: 01 44 51 31 00; *Embassy*: 35 rue du Faubourg-St-Honoré, 8th; tel: 01 44 51 31 00; www.amb-grandebretagne.fr.

US: *Embassy*: Consular Section, 2 avenue Gabriel, 8th; tel: 01 43 12 22 22; https://fr.usembassy.gov.

Emergency numbers

Ambulance (SAMU): tel: 15
Fire brigade *(pompiers)*: tel: 18
Police *(police secours)*: tel: 17
From a mobile phone: tel: 112

Green issues

For information on environmental matters in Paris, visit the news section of www.environnement.paris.fr. When throwing away litter, note that white-lidded bins are for glass, yellow-lidded ones are for everything else recyclable, green bins are for non-recyclable rubbish and brown are for compost.

Health

EU Nationals: If you are an EU national and you fall ill in France, you can receive emergency medical treatment from doctors, dentists and hospitals. You will have to pay the cost of this treatment, but are entitled to claim back up to 70 percent if you have a **European Health Insurance Card** (in the UK. tel: 0300 330 1350;

www.nhs.uk). Post-Brexit, access to healthcare for British citizens visiting an EU country is likely to change. British citizens should continue to buy travel insurance in order to receive any healthcare treatment needed.

North Americans: The International Association for Medical Assistance to Travellers (2162 Gordon Street, Ontario N1L 1G6, Canada; tel: 416-652 0137; www.iamat.org) is a non-profit-making group that offers members fixed rates for medical treatment, a medical record from their doctor and a directory of English-speaking doctors in France. Free membership.

American Hospital (Hôpital Américain de Paris): 63 boulevard Victor-Hugo, Neuilly; tel: 01 46 41 25 25; www.american-hospital.org; metro: Porte Maillot, then bus 82 to the last stop. Private hospital with English-speaking staff.

Pharmacies

Most pharmacies are open from 9 or 10am to 7 or 8pm. At night, they post the addresses of the nearest late-opening pharmacies in their windows. Late-opening pharmacies include **Publicis Drugstore**, 133 avenue des Champs-Élysées, 8th; tel: 01 44 43 75 07; open daily 8am–2am, Sun and Sat from 10am; metro: Charles de Gaulle-Étoile, George V.

Internet

Wi-fi (pronounced "wee-fee" in France) is now widely available in French hotels,

Don't be distracted in Montmartre – be mindful of pickpockets

although some places may charge you for it. For a list of free Wi-fi spots around the city, including public buildings, parks and squares see www.paris.fr. There are cyber cafés all over the city – ask at the tourist office for current ones or see http://en.parisinfo.com.

L

LGBTQ travellers

The Marais (4th *arrondissement*) is the most LGBTQ-friendly district, with LGBTQ-oriented restaurants, wine bars, boutiques, bookshops, beauty salons, hotels, bars and discos. The **Centre Lesbien, Gai, Bi et Trans**: (63 rue Beaubourg, 3rd; tel: 01 43 57 21 47; www.centrelgbtparis.org) houses a lending library and advises on health, social and legal issues.

LGBTQ literature

There are various free magazines you can pick up in LGBTQ bars in the 3rd and 4th *arrondissements*. The magazine *Têtu* (www.tetu.com) is a useful source of information for the LGBTQ community, and can be bought at most news kiosks in the city. Also see www.patroc.com/paris.

Lost property

To reclaim lost items in Paris, go in person (with ID) to the Bureau des Objets Trouvés, 36 rue des Morillons, 15th; tel: 01 53 71 53 71; Mon–Fri 8.30am–4pm, Thu until noon; metro: Convention.

M

Maps

Paris Classique par Arrondissement can usually be found at various newsstands for around €10.

Media

Newspapers: The two main national dailies are *Le Monde*, which has a rather dry and leftish slant, and the more conservative *Le Figaro*. On the far left is the Communist *L'Humanité*, while between that and *Le Monde* is Jean-Paul Sartre's brainchild, *Libération*.

The major weekly news magazines are *Le Point* (right), *L'Express* (centre) and *L'Obs* (left).

To find out what is going on in Paris, buy *L'Officiel des Spectacles* (out on Wednesday; www.offi.fr), with listings of films, clubs, exhibitions, concerts, theatres etc.

Radio: France Inter (87.8 MHz) is the biggest station, offering something to suit all tastes. Radio Classique (101.1 MHz) plays lightweight classical music. For something slightly less mainstream, try France Musiques (91.7 MHz), or RTL (104.3 MHz), which plays chart music interspersed with chat. Europe 1 (104.7 FM) is the best for morning news coverage, while France Info (105.5 FM) broadcasts the news.

Television: TF1, France 2, France 3, France 5/Arte and M6 are the five main television stations. There is also a huge choice of cable channels. Canal+ is a subscription channel, which shows big-name films.

Metro sign

Money

Currency: France uses the euro, divided into 100 cents. Coins *(pièces)* come in 1, 2, 5, 10, 20 and 50 cents, and 1 and 2 euros. Banknotes *(billets)* come in 5, 10, 20, 50, 100, 200 and 500 euros.

Exchange: Bureaux de change at train stations vary their hours in high or low seasons, but most are open Monday to Sat 9/10am–8pm. In banks, separate exchange counters are increasingly rare. Exchange offices at Roissy-Charles de Gaulle (terminals 2A, 2B and 2D) and Orly-Sud airports are typically open longer. Travelex at 194 rue de Rivoli, 1st, tel: 01 47 03 49 52, Mon–Sat 9.15am–7.30pm, Sun 10.45am–5.45pm. For other locations visit: www.travelex.fr. Multi Change at 180 boulevard St-Germain, 6th, tel: 01 42 22 41 00, www.multi-change.com. Mon–Sat 9.30am–6.30pm. Take your passport if you want to cash travellers' cheques.

Cash Machines: The easiest way to take out money is to use an ATM, with a debit or credit card such as Visa, MasterCard, Maestro or Cirrus, etc, and your PIN.

Credit Cards: Most shops, restaurants and hotels accept credit cards.

Post

Post Offices: Main branches are open Mon–Fri 8am–7pm, Sat 8am–noon. The central post office is at 49 Rue la Boétie, 8th; www.laposte.fr.

Public holidays

1 Jan New Year's Day
Mar/Apr Easter Monday
1 May Labour Day
8 May end of World War II in Europe
Mid-/late May Ascension Day
Late May Whit Monday
14 July Bastille Day
15 Aug Feast of the Assumption
1 Nov All Saints' Day
11 Nov Armistice Day, 1918
25 Dec Christmas

Religion

The majority of people in Paris are nominally Roman Catholic, although in practice many are not religious. The *Yellow Pages (Les Pages Jaunes)*, see www.pagesjaunes.fr, lists places of worship for every faith and denomination.

Smoking

Smoking is banned in railway stations, airports, shops and offices, restaurants and bars – with fines in place for anyone flouting the ban.

Stamps

These *(timbres)* are available at most *tabacs* (tobacconists) and other shops selling postcards or greetings cards. For more details and postage costs, visit www.laposte.fr.

In the metro

T

Telephones

Phone Numbers: All telephone numbers in France have 10 digits. Paris and Île-de-France (Paris region) landline numbers begin with 01. Toll-free telephone numbers start 0800; all other numbers beginning 08 (accessible in France only) are charged at variable rates; 06 numbers are for mobile phones. For the operator, call 12.

Calling from Abroad: To dial Paris from the UK: 00 (international code) + 33 (France) + 1 (Paris) + an eight-figure number. To call other countries from France, dial the international code (00), then the country code: Australia 61, UK 44, US and Canada 1.

For US visitors, prepaid phone cards include ATT, Continental and Solaris: see www.comfi.com for details.

Public Telephone Boxes: Phone boxes in Paris are scarce nowadays and they require a card *(télécarte)*, bought from kiosks, *tabacs* and post offices to operate. Certain cafés and *tabacs* may have a public phone; most no longer take coins but you can usually use your credit card.

Time zones

France is one hour ahead of Greenwich Mean Time (GMT) and six ahead of Eastern Standard Time.

Tipping

By law, restaurant bills must include a service charge, which is usually 12 or 15 percent. Nevertheless, it is common to leave a small additional tip (not more than 5 percent) for the waiter if the service has been especially good. Address waiters as *Monsieur* (never *garçon*) and waitresses as *Mademoiselle,* if they are young, or *Madame,* if they are older.

For taxi fares, rounding up to the nearest euro is the norm.

Tour operators

By Boat: Seine cruises last an hour, with commentaries in several languages. In high season, boats leave every half-hour, 10am–9.30pm. **Batobus** is a 'riverbus' service based at Port de la Bourdonnais by the Eiffel Tower (tel: 01 76 64 79 12; www.batobus.com). **Bateaux Mouches** depart from Pont de l'Alma (tel: 01 42 25 96 10; www.bateaux-mouches.fr); **Vedettes du Pont Neuf** depart from Pont Neuf (tel: 01 46 33 98 38; www.vedettes-dupontneuf.com).

Canal Trips: These run along the Canal St-Martin, from the Bastille to the Parc de la Villette and vice versa. Try **Canauxrama** (13 quai de la Loire, 19th; tel: 01 42 39 15 00; www.canauxrama.com) or **Paris Canal** (19/21 quai de la Loire, 19th; tel: 01 42 40 29 00; www.pariscanal.com).

By Coach: Most companies provide a commentary in several languages and pass the major sights, but do not stop along the way. **Big Bus Paris** (English and French; tel: 01 53 953 953; www.bigbustours.com) runs double-decker buses to the main tourist sites. Hop off, sightsee, then catch a later bus. **Paris L'Open Tour** (tel: 01 42 66 56 56; www.paris.

opentour.com), operated by RATP, runs a similar service, also with open-topped double-decker buses.

By 2CV: 4 Roues sous 1 Parapluie (22 rue Bernard, Dimey, 18th; tel: 01 58 59 27 82; www.4roues-sous-1parapluie. com) offers tours of the city in a soft-topped Citroën 2CV (hence the name: four wheels under an umbrella). Each car holds a maximum of three passengers.

Tourist information

In Paris: see http://en.parisinfo.com for details of all services. The branches of the Paris Tourist Office include:

Main Branch: Hôtel de Ville - 29 rue de Rivoli 4st; daily May–Oct 9am–7pm, Nov–Apr 10am–7pm; metro: Hôtel de Ville

Gare du Nord, 18 rue de Dunkerque, 10th; daily 8.30am–6pm; metro: Gare du Nord.

Réception du Carrousel du Louvre (information only), 99 rue de Rivoli, 1st; daily 10am–8pm; metro: Palais Royal-Musée du Louvre

Anvers, 72 boulevard Rochechouart, 18th; daily 10am–6pm; metro: Anvers.

UK: Lincoln House, 296–302 High Holborn, London WC1V 7JH; tel: 44 207 061 66 31; http://uk.france.fr.

US: 825 3rd Avenue, 29 Fl, New York, NY 10022; tel: 212-838 7800; http://us.france.fr.

Canada: 1800 avenue McGill Collège, Bureau 1010, Montréal, Québec H3A 3J6; canada@atout-france.fr; http://ca.france.fr.

Transport

Arrival

By Rail: Eurostar has fast, frequent rail services from London (St Pancras) or Ashford station to Paris (Gare du Nord). The service runs over a dozen times a day and takes just over two hours (two hours from Ashford). For reservations, tel: 03432-186 186 (UK) or 08 92 35 35 39 (France) or visit www.eurostar.com. There are reduced fares for children aged 4–11; under 4s travel free but are not guaranteed a seat.

By Sea: Ferries running from the UK to northern France offer attractive prices in competition with the Channel Tunnel. There are motorway links from Boulogne, Calais and Le Havre to Paris.

By Air: Air France KLM is one of the main agents for flights to France from the US and within Europe. For British travellers, in addition to major airlines (British Airways, etc.), several low-cost airlines including Easyjet, CityJet and Flybe offer flights to Paris from London and other British cities. See www.skyscanner.net for the best deals.

By Car: Eurotunnel takes cars from Folkestone to Calais on the drive-on, drive-off **Le Shuttle**. It takes 35 minutes from platform to platform and about one hour from motorway to motorway. Payment is made at toll booths, which accept cash, cheques or credit cards. The price applies to the car, not the number of passengers.

You can book in advance with Eurotunnel on tel: 08443-353 535 (UK) or 08 10

Traffic on the Champs-Élysées

63 03 04 (France) or at www.eurotunnel.com. You can also just turn up and take the next available service. Le Shuttle runs 24 hours a day, and there are from two to five an hour, depending on the season and time.

By Bus: National Express Eurolines runs services daily from London's Victoria Coach Station to Paris, providing one of the cheaper ways to get there. Discounts are available for young people and senior citizens, and the ticket includes the ferry crossing. For details tel: 08 71 781 8181; www.nationalexpress.com; or Eurolines France, at the Gare Routière-Coach Station Galliéni, 28 avenue du Général de Gaulle, Bagnolet; tel: 08 92 89 90 91; metro Galliéni. See also www.eurolines.fr.

Airports

Roissy-Charles-de-Gaulle: The fastest way of getting to central Paris from Roissy-Charles-de-Gaulle is by RER B train. These leave every 10–20 minutes between around 5am and midnight from terminal 2 and run to the metro at Gare du Nord, Châtelet or Denfert-Rochereau. The journey takes around 25–35 minutes.

The **Roissy** bus runs between the airport and Paris Opéra station from terminals 1, 2 and 3. It runs every 15 minutes 6am–8.45pm, then every 20 minutes until 12.30am. From the Paris Opéra it runs from 5.15am–12.30am, every 15–30 minutes. The **Air France bus** (to metro Porte de Maillot, Arc de Triomphe, Gare de Lyon or Montparnasse) runs every 15–30 minutes from 5.45am to 11pm. Another bus operator, **Le Bus Direct** also offers direct service to Eiffel Tower/Montparnasse area.

By **taxi**, the journey from Charles de Gaulle can take anything from around 30 minutes to over an hour, depending on the traffic. The charge is metered, with supplements payable for each large piece of luggage. An average fare between the airport and central Paris is €50 by day, €60 at night.

Orly: To get to central Paris from Orly, take the **shuttle** from Orly Sud or Orly Ouest to Pont de Rungis railway station. The RER C stops at Austerlitz, Pont St-Michel and Invalides. It runs every 15 minutes from 5am to 11.40pm and takes around 30 minutes to Austerlitz.

Alternatively, the **Orlybus** (to place Denfert-Rochereau) leaves from Orly Sud or Orly Ouest. It runs every 13–20 minutes from 6am to 11.30pm. The more expensive **Orlyval** automatic train is a shuttle to Antony (the nearest RER to Orly). It runs every 7 minutes, 6am–11pm, and takes 35 minutes.

Air France buses (to Eiffel Tower, Trocadéro, Gare Montparnasse, and Arc de Triomphe Champs-Elysées) leave from Orly Sud or Orly Ouest. They run every 15–30 minutes from around 5am to 11.40pm and take anywhere from 25–60 minutes. Tickets are available on board or from their website www.lebusdirect.com.

By **taxi**, the journey from Orly to the city centre takes around 20–40 minutes, depending on the traffic, and cost between €30 and €35.

A bateau-mouche trip on the Seine is a must-do

Transport within Paris

Bus (autobus): Bus transport around Paris is efficient, though not always fast. You can get a bus map from metro station ticket offices. Most buses run 7am–8.30pm, some until 12.30am. Service is reduced on Sundays and public holidays. Some 47 Noctilien lines run from 12.30am–5.30am, with hubs at the Gare de l'Est, Gare Montparnasse, Gare St-Lazare, Châtelet and Gare de Lyon.

Tickets: You can buy a ticket as you board, but it's cheaper to buy a book of tickets *(carnet)* from any metro station or tobacconist. Bus and metro tickets are interchangeable. Punch your ticket in the validating machine when you get on. You can also buy special Paris Visite tourist passes or a Navigo Découverte swipe card (see page 132).

Metro: The Paris Métropolitain is one of the most efficient and least expensive metro systems in the world. Services start at about 5.30am and finish around 1am. The RATP (metro organisation) has an information office at 54 quai de la Rapée, 12th; tel: 34 24 (within France); www.ratp.fr.

Express lines (RER – Réseau Express Régional) get you into the centre of Paris from the suburbs in about 15 minutes, with a few stops in between.

You can buy single tickets or you can get 10 journeys for the discounted price with a carnet (book) of tickets, also valid for the bus network and for the RER, provided that you stay within Paris and don't go to outer suburbs. Make sure to keep your ticket with you for the duration of your journey.

A **Paris Visite** ticket, valid for one, two, three or five days, for 1–3 or 1–5 zones (the latter includes airport links and travel to Disneyland Resort Paris and Versailles), allows unlimited travel on the bus, suburban trains, RER, trams or metro, and reductions on entrance fees to various attractions. A day ticket, **Forfait 1 Jour Mobilis**, is valid for the metro, RER, buses, suburban trains and some airport buses.

For longer stays, the best buy is a **Navigo Découverte** swipe card. It costs from €5 for the card itself (and you'll need a passport photograph), which can then be topped up to make it into either a weekly *(hebdomadaire)* Mon–Sun, or monthly *(mensuel)* card – the latter dates from the first of the month. The Navigo card allows unlimited rides inside Paris on the metro, RER, suburban train, trams and buses including the Orly and Roissy-Charles de Gaulle airports, Versailles and Disneyland.

Train: The SNCF (French Railways Authority) runs fast, comfortable trains on an efficient network. The high-speed service (TGV – *train à grande vitesse*). See www.sncf.com or www.voyages-sncf.com; tel: 36 35 (in France).

Taxi: An unoccupied cab can be recognised by an illuminated white sign on its roof. Fares differ according to the zones covered or the time of the day (you'll be charged more between 5pm and 7am and on Sunday), and there are extra charges for putting luggage in the boot and for pick-up at a station or airport. Taxi drivers can refuse to carry more than three passengers. The fourth, if admitted, pays a supplement.

Tour group at the Louvre

The following taxi companies take phone bookings 24 hours a day:
Alpha: 01 45 85 85 85
G7: 36 07
Taxi in Paris: 9 77 21 72 72

Car rental

To hire a car you will need to show your driving licence (held for at least a year) and passport. You will also need a major credit card, or a large deposit. The minimum age for renting cars is 21, although a young driver's supplement is usually payable for those under 25. Third-party insurance is compulsory, and full cover is recommended.

The international car-hire firms operating in Paris include: **Avis** (tel: 08 21 23 07 60; www.avis.fr), **Europcar/National/InterRent** (tel: 08 25 35 83 58; www.europcar.fr) and **Hertz** (tel: 01 39 38 38 38; www.hertz.fr).

Parking: Street parking is hard to find; spaces are usually controlled until 8pm by pay-and-display machines (*horodateurs*). Most car parks are underground (visit www.parkingsdeparis.fr).

Petrol (Gas): This can be hard to track down in the city centre, so if your tank is almost empty head for a *porte* (exit) on the Périphérique (the multi-lane ring road), where there are stations open 24 hours a day all year round.

Travellers with disabilities

Travellers with mobility problems are advised to book accommodation in advance. Official hotel lists use a symbol to denote wheelchair access, but it's a good idea to check with the hotel regarding the exact facilities available. Information on hotels with good access facilities can be found on the Paris Tourist Office website, http://en.parisinfo.com.

Hotels in the Accor group (www.accorhotels.com) and Louvre Hotels group (www.louvrehotels.com) have at least one room for disabled guests in a variety of chains to suit all budgets.

French Organisations: Association des Paralysés de France, 13 place de Rungis, 13th; tel: 01 53 80 92 97; www.apf-francehandicap.org.

UK Organisations: Disability Rights UK, 14 East Bay Lane, Here East, Queen Elizabeth Olympic Park, Stratford, London; tel: 0330 995 0400; www.disabilityrightsuk.org.

US Organisations: Society for Accessible Travel and Hospitality (SATH), tel: 212-447 7284; www.sath.org.

Visas

Visitors from outside of the European Schengen area are required to carry a valid passport. No visa is required by visitors from the EU, the US, Australia, Canada, or New Zealand. Nationals of other countries may need a visa; if in doubt (and, advisably, if visiting for over 90 days), check with the French Consulate in your home country.

A typical menu

LANGUAGE

In general, if you attempt to communicate in French, the fact that you have made an effort is likely to break the ice and win favour with Parisians.

General

yes *oui*
no *non*
please *s'il vous plaît*
thank you (very much) *merci (beaucoup)*
you're welcome *de rien*
excuse me *excusez-moi*
hello *bonjour*
hi/bye *salut*
goodbye *au revoir*
good evening *bonsoir*
How much is it? *C'est combien?*
What is your name? *Comment vous appelez-vous?*
My name is... *Je m'appelle...*
Do you speak English? *Parlez-vous anglais?*
I am English/American *Je suis Anglais(e)/ Américain(e)*
I don't understand *Je ne comprends pas*
Please speak more slowly *Parlez plus lentement, s'il vous plaît*
Can you help me? *Pouvez-vous m'aider?*
I'm looking for... *Je cherche...*
Where is...? *Où est...?*
I'm sorry *Excusez-moi/Pardon*
I don't know *Je ne sais pas*
Have a good day! *Bonne journée!*
See you soon *A bientôt*
When? *Quand?*

What time is it? *Quelle heure est-il?*
here *ici*
there *là*
left *gauche*
right *droite*
straight on *tout droit*
far *loin*
near *près d'ici*
opposite *en face*
beside *à côté de*
over there *là-bas*
today *aujourd'hui*
yesterday *hier*
tomorrow *demain*
now *maintenant*
later *plus tard*
this morning *ce matin*
this afternoon *cet après-midi*
this evening *ce soir*

Getting around

I want to get off at... *Je voudrais descendre à…*
Which line do I take for...? *Quelle ligne dois-je prendre pour...?*
Validate your ticket *Compostez votre billet*
airport *l'aéroport*
railway station *la gare*
bus station *la gare routière*
metro stop *la station de métro*
bus *l'autobus, le car*
bus stop *l'arrêt*
platform *le quai*
ticket *le billet*
return ticket *aller-retour*

Parisian lights

Emergencies

Help! *Au secours!*
Stop! *Arrêtez!*
Where is the nearest telephone? *Où est le téléphone le plus proche?*
Where is the nearest hospital? *Où est l'hôpital le plus proche?*
I am sick *Je suis malade*
I have lost my passport/ purse *J'ai perdu mon passeport/porte-monnaie*

Shopping

I'd like to buy *Je voudrais acheter*
How much is it? *C'est combien?*
Do you take credit cards? *Est-ce que vous acceptez les cartes de crédit?*
I'm just looking *Je regarde seulement*
size (clothes) *la taille*
size (shoes) *la pointure*
receipt *le reçu*

Sightseeing

tourist information office *l'office du tourisme*
free *gratuit*
open *ouvert*
closed *fermé*
every day *tous les jours*
all year *toute l'année*
all day *toute la journée*
to book *réserver*
town map *le plan*
road map *la carte*

Dining out

breakfast *le petit-déjeuner*
lunch *le déjeuner*
dinner *le dîner*

meal *le repas*
first course *l'entrée*
main course *le plat principal*
drink included *boisson comprise*
wine list *la carte des vins*
the bill *l'addition*
I am a vegetarian *Je suis végétarien(ne)*
I'd like to order *Je voudrais commander*
service included *service compris*

Online communications

Does it have wireless internet? *Est-ce qu'il a la connexion Wi-Fi?*
What is the Wi-Fi password? *Quel est le mot de passe du Wi-Fi?*
Is the Wi-fi free? *Est-ce que le WiFi est gratuit ?*
Do you have bluetooth? *Avez-vous Bluetooth ?*
Can I...? *Puis-je...?*
...access the internet *accéder à Internet*
...check my e-mail *consulter mes mails*
...print *imprimer*
...access Skype? *accéder à Skype?*

Social media

Are you on Facebook/Twitter/Instagram? *Etes-vous sur Facebook/Twitter/Instagram?*
What's your user name? *Quel est votre nom d'utilisateur ?*
I'll add you as a friend. *Je vous ajouterai comme ami.*
I'll follow you on Twitter/Instagram. *Je vous suivrai sur Twitter/Instagram.*
I'll put the pictures on Facebook/Twitter/Instagram. *Je mettrai les photos sur Facebook/Twitter/Instagram.*

BOOKS AND FILM

Books

François Villon's bawdy medieval poetry, the 19th-century realist novels of Victor Hugo or Honoré de Balzac, the Symbolist poetry of Charles Baudelaire and the Existentialist novels of Jean-Paul Sartre are just a few of the literary works that have taken inspiration from the city of Paris across the centuries.

History
A Concise History of France, by Roger Price. Excellent historical overview.
Marie Antoinette, by Antonia Fraser. An interesting biography of France's most famous queen.
Parisians: An Adventure History of Paris, by Graham Robb. A fascinating look at the individuals who shaped the city.
Sylvia Beach and the Lost Generation: A History of Literary Paris in the Twenties and Thirties, by Noel Riley Fitch. The origins of Shakespeare & Company bookshop and the writers who went there.

Art and architecture
A Propos de Paris, by Henri Cartier-Bresson. Some 130 stunning black-and-white photographs of Paris, spanning 50 years.
The Cathedral Builders, by Jean Gimpel. The story of the hands and minds behind the cathedrals of France.
Paris: An Architectural History, by Anthony Sutcliffe. A great book on the architecture of the capital across the ages.

Paris: Art and Architecture by Martina Padberg. A comprehensive guide to the city's art and architecture from its origins to the 21st century.
Robert Doisneau: Paris. A compact book featuring more than 600 of the photographer's images of Paris.

Expat memoirs
A Moveable Feast, by Ernest Hemingway. Life with the literati in 1920s Paris.
A Year in the Merde, by Stephen Clarke. The best-selling humorous tale of an expat in Paris.
My life in France, by Julia Child. Magical memoir of Julia Child's years in France.

Fiction
Murder in the Palais Royal, by Cara Black. One of a series of entertaining crime novels set in and around Paris.
The Elegance of the Hedgehog, by Muriel Barbery. A moving tale of a friendship between a young girl and the concierge of her apartment building.
The Sun King Rises, by Yves Jégo and Denis Lépée. Intrigue and mystery in the court of Louis XIV.

Food
Paris Bistro Cooking, by Linda Dannenberg. Tasty dishes from a wealth of Paris brasseries.
The Little Paris Kitchen, by Rachel Khoo. Easy-to-make versions of French classics.

Paris has inspired countless books and films

The Paris Café Cookbook, by Daniel Young. Recipes and excerpts on recommended cafés in the capital.

The Sweet Life in Paris, by David Lebovitz. The Paris-based American chef's observations on Paris and cooking, including 50 recipes.

Films

If Paris feels eternally familiar, thank the movies. Indeed, you're in film-set Paris the second you get off the train at the Gare du Nord, filmed by Orson Welles (**F for Fake**), amongst many others.

Next, naturally, you make your way to the métro – an ever popular film location, used by everyone from Henri-Georges Clouzot to the Coen brothers. Perhaps you come out at the Champs-Elysées – another classic setting; as you walk up, imagine the Wehrmacht's daily parade coming the other way, as recreated to sobering effect in Jean-Pierre Melville's **L'Armée des Ombres** (1969). Or retrace Jean Seberg and Jean-Paul Belmondo's steps as they walk down the famous avenue in probably the most famous Paris film, Jean-Luc Godard's **Breathless** (**A Bout de Souffle**; 1960).

And it's hard to miss the Eiffel Tower: not only filmed more times than it has rivets (the pioneering Lumière brothers were first – their 1900 portrait of the 11-year-old tower is still extant), it even starred in its own cartoon, **Bonjour Paris**.

Hollywood has long been enchanted by the City of Light, from the 1950s films **An American in Paris**, starring Gene Kelly, and **Funny Face**, featuring Audrey Hepburn, to the controversial 1970s Marlon Brando movie **Last Tango in Paris** and Woody Allen's time-travelling 2011 offering, **Midnight in Paris**. And the 2006 anthology **Paris, je t'aime (Paris, I love you)**, featuring a flurry of European and Hollywood actors, is made up of 22 short films each set in a different *arrondissement*.

More recently, Paris featured in Michael Haneke's **Amour** and **Holy Motors** by Léos Carax (both 2012), **Something in the Air** by Olivier Assayas (2013) and **120 Beats Per Minute** by Robin Campillo (2017).

For a slice of the gritty life in the *banlieues* that surround Paris, Matthieu Kassovitz's ferocious 1995 agitprop drama **La Haine** (1995) is still all too relevant. At the other end of the spectrum is Jean-Pierre Jeunet's 2001 smash hit **Amélie (Le Fabuleux Destin d'Amélie Poulain)**, a sugary-sweet nostalgic tale of villagey Paris.

New Wave

When people think of Paris movies, they often have in mind a small clutch of films – including **Breathless** and **The 400 Blows** – made by a small group of people in a short space of time. These Nouvelle Vague ("new wave") films were made between the late 1950s and mid-1960s, by a loosely affiliated group of directors opposed to what they saw as the stuffiness of cinema of the day; its leading figures were Jean-Luc Godard, François Truffaut, Claude Chabrol, Eric Rohmer and Jacques Rivette. One of the movement's few women directors was Agnès Varda, whose 1962 film **Cléo de 5 à 7** is one of the best of the bunch.

ABOUT THIS BOOK

This *Explore Guide* has been produced by the editors of Insight Guides, whose books have set the standard for visual travel guides since 1970. With top-quality photography and authoritative recommendations, these guidebooks bring you the very best routes and itineraries in the world's most exciting destinations.

BEST ROUTES

The routes in the book provide something to suit all budgets, tastes and trip lengths. As well as covering the destination's many classic attractions, the itineraries track lesser-known sights, and there are also ex-cursions for those who want to extend their visit outside the city. The routes embrace a range of interests, so whether you are an art fan, a gourmet, a history buff or have kids to entertain, you will find an option to suit.

We recommend reading the whole of a route before setting out. This should help you to familiarise yourself with it and enable you to plan where to stop for refreshments – options are shown in the 'Food and Drink' box at the end of each tour.

For our pick of the tours by theme, consult Recommended Routes for… (see pages 6–7).

INTRODUCTION

The routes are set in context by this introductory section, giving an overview of the destination to set the scene, plus background information on food and drink, shopping and more, while a succinct history timeline highlights the key events over the centuries.

DIRECTORY

Also supporting the routes is a Directory chapter, with a clearly organised A–Z of practical information, our pick of where to stay while you are there and select restaurant listings; these eateries complement the more low-key cafés and restaurants that feature within the routes and are intended to offer a wider choice for evening dining. Also included here are some nightlife listings, plus a handy language guide and our recommendations for books and films about the destination.

ABOUT THE AUTHORS

Victoria Trott is a freelance travel writer who specialises in France. A graduate in French and Spanish from Leeds University, she contributes to a wide variety of publications and has written or updated guidebooks for most major travel publishers. Her first visit to Paris didn't go too well: it rained every day and she got lost every time she used the metro. However, after being seduced by cake shops and the bygone charm of the Latin Quarter, Paris is now her favourite city. This book builds on original content by Michael Macaroon.

CONTACT THE EDITORS

We hope you find this Explore Guide useful, interesting and a pleasure to read. If you have any questions or feedback on the text, pictures or maps, please do let us know. If you have noticed any errors or outdated facts, or have suggestions for places to include on the routes, we would be delighted to hear from you. Please drop us an email at hello@insightguides.com. Thanks!

CREDITS

Explore Paris
Managing Editor: Carine Tracanelli
Author: Michael Macaroon, Victoria Trott
Picture Editors: Tom Smyth & Aude Vauconsant
Layout: Aga Bylica
Update Production: Apa Digital
Cartography: original cartography Berndtson & Berndston GmbH, updated by Carte
Photo credits: Alamy 16/17, 33L, 73, 77, 83, 84, 86, 86/87, 87L, 90, 101L, 102/103T, 107L, 109, 114, 116, 118, 119L, 118/119, 120; Apa Publications 44/45; Corbis 23; Disneyland Paris 100/101; Dreamstime.com 6MC, 100; Fotolia 96; Getty Images 1, 4/5T, 8/9T, 10, 22, 24/25T, 42, 50, 54, 55L, 76, 80/81, 91, 106/107, 115L, 123; Ilpo Musto/ Apa Publications 12B, 13, 14, 34/35, 60, 79L, 81L, 93L, 94, 95, 127; iStock 4MR, 4MR, 4ML, 4MC, 7M, 8MC, 8MR, 19L, 18/19, 26, 28, 32, 41L, 51, 53, 54/55, 57, 65L, 71L, 78/79, 82, 97, 98, 99L, 124, 125, 128, 129, 130/131, 132, 134, 135; Kevin Cummins/Apa Publications 4ML, 7T, 7MR, 8ML, 8ML, 8MC, 8MR, 12T, 24MC, 31, 45L, 61, 63, 64, 74, 80, 102ML, 102MR, 102MC, 102ML, 104/105, 121, 122, 126, 133; Leonardo 112/113; Lydia Evans/Rough Guides 20, 102MC; Mathieu Rainaud/Monsieur Bleu 72; Ming Tang-Evans/ Apa Publications 6ML, 6BC, 7MR, 11, 16, 17L, 18, 21, 24MR, 24MR, 24MC, 24MC, 27, 30, 32/33, 35L, 36, 37, 38, 38/39, 39L, 40, 40/41, 44, 46, 47L, 46/47, 48, 49, 52, 56, 58, 59, 64/65, 66, 67L, 68, 69L, 68/69, 70, 70/71, 78, 88/89, 89L, 102MR, 106, 110/111, 114/115, 117, 136/137; Public domain 34, 92, 98/99; Shutterstock 4MC, 6TL, 15, 24MC, 29, 43, 62, 66/67, 74/75, 85, 88, 92/93; Terrass 108
Cover credits: Luigi Vaccarella/4Corners Images (main) iStock (bottom)
Printed by CTPS – China

All Rights Reserved
© 2019 Apa Digital (CH) AG and
Apa Publications (UK) Ltd

Third Edition 2019

DISTRIBUTION

UK, Ireland and Europe
Apa Publications (UK) Ltd
sales@insightguides.com
United States and Canada
Ingram Publisher Services
ips@ingramcontent.com
Australia and New Zealand
Woodslane
info@woodslane.com.au
Southeast Asia
Apa Publications (Singapore) Pte
singaporeoffice@insightguides.com
Worldwide
Apa Publications (UK) Ltd
sales@insightguides.com

SPECIAL SALES, CONTENT LICENSING AND COPUBLISHING

Insight Guides can be purchased in bulk quantities at discounted prices. We can create special editions, personalised jackets and corporate imprints tailored to your needs.
sales@insightguides.com
www.insightguides.biz

INDEX

MAP LEGEND

● Start of tour

→ Tour & route direction

❶ Recommended sight

❷ Recommended
   restaurant/café

★ Place of interest

ℹ Tourist information

Ⓜ Ⓡ Metro / RER station

⚊ Statue/monument

✉ Main post office

🚌 Main bus station

- - - Ferry route

- - - National park boundry

·- - - Regional boundary

    Park

    Important building

    Hotel

    Transport hub

    Shopping / market

    Pedestrian area

    Urban area

    Marsh

INSIGHT ⊙ GUIDES

OFF THE SHELF

Since 1970, INSIGHT GUIDES has provided a unique perspective on the world's best travel destinations by using specially commissioned photography and illuminating text written by local authors.

Whether you're planning a city break, a walking tour or the journey of a lifetime, our superb range of guidebooks and phrasebooks will inspire you to discover more about your chosen destination.

INSIGHT GUIDES

offer a unique combination of stunning photos, absorbing narrative and detailed maps, providing all the inspiration and information you need.

PHRASEBOOKS & DICTIONARIES

help users to feel at home, when away. Pocket-sized with a free app to download, they go where you do.

CITY GUIDES

pack hundreds of great photos into a smaller format with detailed practical information, so you can navigate the world's top cities with confidence.

EXPLORE GUIDES

feature easy-to-follow walks and itineraries in the world's most exciting destinations, with our choice of the best places to eat and drink along the way.

POCKET GUIDES

combine concise information on where to go and what to do in a handy compact format, ideal on the ground. Includes a full-colour, fold-out map.

EXPERIENCE GUIDES

feature offbeat perspectives and secret gems for experienced travellers, with a collection of over 100 ideas for a memorable stay in a city.

www.insightguides.com